THISTLE EATERS GUIDE

by r. e. scammell

THISTLE EATERS GUIDE

— THIRD EDITION —

Published by
Floreat Press, 2748 9th Street, Berkeley, California

Printing, platework and binding by
Consolidated Printers, Inc., Berkeley, California

Author's Note

Have you ever eaten a thistle? You have if you've eaten an artichoke! This vegetable has an unusual appeal all of its own—a unique delicate nut-like flavor which makes it nice to eat.

The botanical name of the artichoke is Cynara Scolymus. The common name "artichoke" is derived from the northern Italian words "articiocco" and "articoclos." The latter term is supposed to have evolved from the Liqurian word "cocal," meaning pine cone, which aptly describes the buds of an artichoke plant. Someone once said that an artichoke looks like a pine cone attempting to be a cabbage.

The artichoke is such a spectacular vegetable that there are endless opportunities to enjoy it: from a picturesque field of purple-violet artichoke blooms; served in a salad or as a main course; or dried blooms used as decorations.

The following anthology of recipes have been compiled to introduce you to this much-neglected and centuries-old delicacy.

Avant-Propos

According to an Aegean legend and praised in song by the poet Quintus Horatius Flaccus, the first artichoke was a lovely young girl who lived on the island Zinari and who was changed into an artichoke by an angry god jealous of her beauty.

The artichoke is believed to be a native of the Mediterranean region and the Canary Islands. Its origin dates back to the time of the Greek philosopher and naturalist Theophrastus, (371-287 B.C.) who wrote of them being grown in Italy and Sicily.

Artichokes were first cultivated at Naples around the middle of the 15th century, and gradually spread to other sections of Europe. In Horace's Rome, they were the most expensive of all garden produce and were preserved in vinegar, or brine, or with laserwort root and cumin. This enabled the rich to enjoy them all year round. Throughout the world today artichokes are still preserved much the same manner. After the fall of the Roman Empire, the artichoke disappeared with the grandeur that was Rome. It was forgotten so completely that Venice, in 1473, acclaimed it as a gastronomic phenomenon. The artichoke was established in Florence during the 1400's in time for Catherine de Medici to take it with her to France. Catherine's favourite dish is said to have been "Fonds d'artichauts." It was under her championship that the artichoke achieved and still holds its mark among gourmets.

How the first artichoke arrived in North America is unknown, but as far back as 1605, the French explorer Samuel de Champlain, discovered that they were grown by Indians in the Cape Cod area. They were further established in Louisiana by French colonists and in the Monterey area of California by the Spaniards during the late 1800's.

At the beginning of the 20th century, commercial growing of artichokes was established in the mid-coastal areas of California where the cool, foggy and relatively frost free climate is perfect for quality production. Castroville, located south of San Francisco, is known as the "Artichoke Center of the World" and each year since 1959 an "Annual Artichoke Festival" is held there during

7

the month of September. Today more than 10,000 acres are under cultivation within seven California counties ranging from Santa Barbara north to Sonoma. The yield per acre varies greatly, depending on the market demand and the weather. Some growers have averaged 20,000 buds per acre. Artichokes are at their best during early winter and reach their most plentiful supply during March and April. Throughout the world today, Italy, France, Spain and the United States are the largest producers of commercially grown and processed artichokes.

There are several varieties of artichokes grown throughout the world. Globular shaped varieties, none of which are grown commercially, include the Red Dutch, White Globe, and Giant Bud. In European countries and Australia varieties with conical shaped buds known as Violet Artichoke, Prickly Artichoke, and Green French Artichoke are grown commercially. In this book we will be dealing with a globular variety known as the Green Globe. This is the only variety produced commercially in California.

Two vegetables which are sometimes thought by name to be a form of Globe artichoke are the Jerusalem and the Chinese artichokes. The Jerusalem artichoke is the edible tuberous root of the same sunflower family as the Globe, and resembles this plant only in flavor. The Indians of North and South America used to cultivate this plant for food, therefore, its origin obviously is not Jerusalem. The origin of the name "Jerusalem" artichoke is unknown, but thought by some to have been derived from the Italian word "Girasole" meaning sunflower. The Chinese artichoke, which also has an edible root, is a native of Northern China and bears no resemblance to the Globe variety.

The artichoke is a perennial in the thistle group of the sunflower (Compositae) family and in full growth the plant spreads to cover an area about six feet in diameter and reaches a height of three to four feet. The long, arching lobed leaves, silver-green in color make the artichoke look much like a giant fern. The buds, if allowed to flower, are up to seven inches in diameter and are a beautiful purple-violet. Nothing is more picturesque than an artichoke field in bloom.

Since artichokes are perennials, the more care in preparing the soil and planting, the better their quality and the greater the harvest. A well cared for plant will produce as many as forty or fifty buds. They grow best in sun, in a deep, rich, loose, well-drained soil. They are a cool weather plant and usually produce their best crop before the arrival of summer's heat. Cool coastal areas are usually best for growing artichokes so the floral development will be slow and the buds will be of high quality. This is not a plant for intermountain areas, but they have been seen in Arizona. If grown in the interior valleys, they should be in the shade as much as possible and will require a lot of water.

March is the time to plant artichokes in Western gardens. They are a fairly large plant, requiring more room than beans or tomatoes, but handsome enough to incorporate in your landscaping plans. These plants can be grown in rows as garden dividers or informal hedges, or grouped together and used to form a wide border.

Plants can be purchased at most nurseries, started from seed, or by dividing the old clumps and planting the offshoots or divisions about six inches deep. The tops should be above ground level. Space each plant three to four feet apart in rows and leave four to five feet between rows—water deeply. Each plant will send up seasonal shoots, the number varies from a single shoot in young plants to as many as 12 or more in plants that are 4 or more years old. Each shoot forms a cluster of large leaves from which a center stem grows. Buds are produced terminally on the elongated stem and on lateral branches. The terminal bud is usually the largest and the lower buds are gradually smaller in size. The buds are ready for harvest when the top bud is about 2 to 4 inches in diameter and still fairly compact. Buds should be cut with about one-and-a-half inches of stem. The yield from three or four plants should be quite enough for a small family's enjoyment. And once established an artichoke plant will provide you with healthy crops from four to seven years.

After harvest, cut back old bearing stalks to ground level and mulch with rotted manure, or feed with a balanced fertilizer. New shoots, which grow from the base of the old stump, will develop their own stalks. Monthly applications of nitrogen fertilizer are beneficial for healthy growth.

In cold winter areas, after the fall harvest, cover the crown of the plant with the leaves. Over this, heap about one foot of some loose mulch, such as straw. Remove in March or April, after the frosts have passed.

Buying & Preparation

When shopping for artichokes, look for ones which are bright green and have tightly packed leaves, (also called bracts). The maturity of an artichoke should not be judged by its size as large artichokes grow on the top of a central stem while medium and small artichokes grow in the middle of the plant on side branches off the main stem and tiny artichokes grow near the base of the plant.

Large artichokes with brown spots or splitting tips and leaves beginning to open, have usually been "winter kist" (damaged by frost) or are older than the tighter buds. Artichokes that have this appearance are still good eating and should not be neglected.

To store fresh artichokes, put them, unwashed, in a plastic bag and refrigerate. They will keep approximately two to three weeks. Artichokes can also be frozen for sometime without impairing their flavor. To prepare them for freezing, trim about 1 inch from the top and trim the stems, then blanch for eight or ten minutes in a mixture of 3 tablespoons citric acid crystals or 1/2 cup lemon juice to each quart of water. Cool quickly in chilled water for 6 to 15 minutes, drain and pack. After blanching, they may be stuffed before freezing.

Recipes that require artichoke hearts or bottoms can be simplified as these items can be purchased at most grocery stores or delicatessen. They appear in glass jars prepared in a marinade oil or brine, or convenient packages of frozen hearts or bottoms.

The artichoke buds contain minerals and vitamins including Calcium, Vitamin A, Thiamine (Vitamin B1), Ascorbic Acid (Vitamin C), Riboflavin, and Protein. Yet with all this nutritive value, there are only 365 calories per pound of edible portion.

An artichoke has four main parts that will be referred to in the recipes: **outer leaves** (first two or three layers usually discarded); **the choke** (the portion that becomes the purple bloom), in small artichokes, as pictured, this portion can be eaten, in large or over-

11

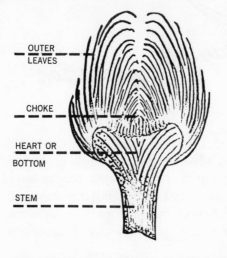

OUTER LEAVES

CHOKE

HEART OR BOTTOM

STEM

mature artichokes, the choke is usually removed; **the heart** or **bottom** consists of the lower section and unformed choke in young artichokes.

Older artichokes can be stripped of the leaves and fluffy choke leaving the large bottom section which is considered by some as the best eating and the **stem** (which is usually trimmed close to the base and discarded).

HOW TO EAT A WHOLE ARTICHOKE

Pull the leaves off one at a time, dip the base of each leaf in the sauce of your choice and nibble off the fleshy end, then discard rest of the leaf. (Use your fingers for this operation.) When all the outer leaves are removed, you come to the tiny undeveloped leaves growing out of the bottom. Pull these off and discard them, and with a knife cut out the fluffy choke underneath. This exposes the most delectable part of the artichoke—the heart or bottom. Cut this in bite-size pieces with your fork, spear each one, dip it in a sauce of your choice and eat.

Most gourmets agree that water should be served with artichokes rather than wine, for wine tasted directly after eating artichokes loses its delicacy, whereas milk or water seems to have a strange pleasing sweetness. If wine is a must at your table, then serve a chilled, dry, robust, white wine such as a Macon, or a chilled, lusty rose such as a Tavel.

METHOD 1—BASIC PREPARATION

Prepare artichokes for cooking by first washing them and trimming the stems to a length of about one inch. Remove any discolored outer leaves and trim off the thorny tips of each leaf with a scissors. Place trimmed artichokes in acidified water to prevent discoloration. Acidified water consists of 1 tablespoon vinegar or lemon juice per quart of water.

Do not use cast-iron utensils at any time in preparation or cooking as this will turn the artichokes black.

Boiled:

Immerse artichokes in a large kettle of boiling salted water allowing at least 1/4 teaspoon of salt for each artichoke. Cover and boil until tender, from 15 to 45 minutes, depending upon the size of the artichokes. Allow 15 to 20 minutes for small artichokes. When they are tender, the leaves may be pulled off easily or the stem can be pierced easily with a fork. Remove them from the water and turn upside down to drain.

Steamed:

Place the artichokes in 1-inch of boiling water, or on a trivet above 1 to 2 inches of boiling water. Sprinkle 1/4 teaspoon salt over each artichoke. Cover closely and cook as for boiled artichokes, but allow 10 to 25 minutes more cooking time. Be careful not to let water boil away as this will cause the artichokes to dry out.

Any one or a combination of the following ingredients may be added to the cooking water: a clove of garlic, 2 tablespoons olive or salad oil, 2 tablespoons lemon juice or red wine vinegar, a few lemon slices or 1 to 2 bay leaves.

Whole Cooked Artichoke for Stuffing:

After the artichoke has drained, hold in hand and gently press top center leaves inward with thumb. This will force the leaves to flower outward. Remove small center leaves and choke. Gently continue spreading leaves to form a cup.

METHOD 2—ARTICHOKE HEARTS

Use medium or small artichokes for preparing hearts. Before cooking, remove the tough outer leaves (about the first three layers) until the light green leaves appear. Cut off top one-quarter and trim stem close to the bottom. Place trimmed hearts in acidified water until ready for cooking. If recipe calls for **cooked hearts, place** hearts in salted boiling water to cover, in which juice of 1/2 lemon and 1 clove garlic have been added. Cover, cook for 15 to 20 minutes or until tender.

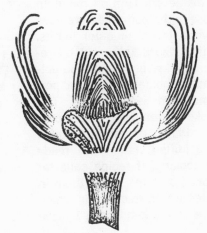

Recipes that require artichoke hearts or bottoms can be simplified as these items can be purchased at most grocery stores or delicatessens. They appear in glass jars prepared in a marinade oil or brine, or convenient packages of frozen hearts or bottoms.

METHOD 3—CASINGS FOR CASSEROLES

Large or medium artichokes are best for stuffing. Before cooking, remove the tough outer leaves (about the first three layers) until the light green leaves appear. Turn artichoke upside down

and press down firmly, this will help the leaves separate. Cut off the top half of the large artichokes and top third of medium artichokes, trim the stem flush to the bottom so it has a flat surface on which to stand. Using a small spoon or melon-baller, scoop out the fibrous center leaves and the fuzzy choke. After removal of the choke, the leaves can be spread further apart with your fingers. Place the prepared casings in acidified water until ready for cooking.

METHOD 4—COOKED CASINGS FOR STUFFING

Boil artichokes in plenty of salted water for about one-half hour until the undersides feel soft when pricked with a fork. (The time will depend on the size of the artichokes.) Drain; cool to room temperature. Discard all the leaves (the large leaves may be scraped and the pulp used in other ways). Carefully separate leaves in center and remove fibrous center choke. Remove first three outer layers of leaves.

METHOD 5—ARTICHOKE BOTTOMS

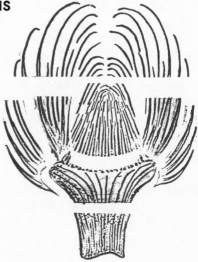

Use the largest artichokes you can find (about 4-1/2 inches in diameter). Trim off the stem close to the bottom and remove several layers of outer leaves. With a sharp knife, cut off remaining leaves flush to the bottom. Immediately rub cut portions with lemon juice. The choke is removed after cooking. Place prepared bottoms in acidified water until ready for cooking. If recipe calls for cooked bottoms, place them in salted water, to cover, in which juice of 1/2 lemon and 1 clove

14

of garlic have been added. Cover and cook for 15 to 20 minutes or until tender. Frozen or bottled artichokes may be substituted.

METHOD 6—ARTICHOKE PULP

Cook large artichokes by Method 1. Scrape the fleshy part from the base of the leaves with a knife, and rub the bottoms through a sieve or food mill.

Pulp may also be made by putting pre-cooked hearts in a blender, at high speed for approximately 30 seconds.

Six large articokes will make about 1-1/2 cups of pulp.

Vegetable

Served alone as a main vegetable dish or accompanied by any number of other vegetables, artichokes will enhance and add interest to most entrees.

ARTICHOKE HEARTS ELEGANTE

1   package frozen artichokes
1   tsp. dried minced onion, dehydrated
1   clove of garlic, crushed
1   tbsp. chopped parsley or 1/2 tbsp. dried parsley
1/2 cup dry bread crumbs
1   tsp. salt
    Freshly ground pepper
1/4 cup olive oil
2   tbsp. water
4   tbsp. grated Parmesan or Romano cheese

Cook artichokes in boiling salted water for 5 minutes; drain well. Place in buttered baking dish. Mix all remaining ingredients; sprinkle over artichokes. Bake at 400° F. for 20 minutes or until soft.

Serves 4.

RICOTTA MUSHROOM STUFFING

8   large artichokes
1-1/2 cups chopped mushrooms
1   slice white bread, broken in small pieces
1/2 tbsp. chopped parsley
2   eggs
1   cup Ricotta cheese
    Grated Parmesan cheese
    Olive oil
    Salt and pepper to taste

Prepare artichokes according to Method 3. Combine mushrooms, bread, garlic, parsley, eggs, ricotta, salt and pepper; and mix together well. Fill artichoke casings with stuffing, heaping stuffing on top. Sprinkle with grated cheese. Arrange artichokes in a greased baking pan (use olive oil) and bake in 350° oven for 30 minutes.

Serves 6.

ARTICHOKE HEART - MUSHROOM BAKE

1 package frozen artichoke hearts
Salad oil, about 1/4 cup
2 medium cloves garlic, minced
1/2 small onion, chopped fine
2 tbsp. minced parsley
Salt and pepper
6-8 fresh mushrooms
1 tsp. lemon juice, optional
6-8 small wedges of tomato, optional

Use a shallow baking pan with a cover, or fit aluminum foil for a cover. Pour in enough salad oil to cover the bottom of the pan, add garlic, onion and parsley. Sprinkle with salt and pepper. Arrange artichoke hearts, cut sides down. Cut mushrooms in half lengthwise and arrange among the hearts. Sprinkle with lemon juice. Brush tops with more oil, sprinkle again with salt and pepper. Cover and bake in moderate oven (350°) for 15 to 30 minutes. If tomato wedges are used, add them the last 10 minutes of baking time.

Serves 4.

EASY SCALLOPED ARTICHOKES

1 small onion, chopped fine
1/4 medium green pepper, chopped fine
2 tbsp. fat or oil
1 package frozen artichoke hearts, cooked
1 egg
3/4 cup sour cream
1/8 tsp. thyme, optional
1/4 tsp. salt
1/8 tsp. sweet basil or rosemary, optional
Dash of hot sauce, optional
8 to 10 small butter crackers

Prepare artichokes according to package directions. Cook onion and green pepper in fat or oil until soft, but not browned. Turn into 1-quart casserole and add artichoke hearts. Beat egg slightly and combine with sour cream. Add seasonings. Pour over artichoke hearts. Crush crackers and sprinkle over top. Bake in moderate oven (350°) for 20 to 25 minutes.

Serves 4.

ARTICHOKE SUPREME

1 package frozen artichoke hearts, cooked
1/2 cup mushrooms
1 cup cooked peas
1/4 tsp. salt
Sprinkle of allspice

Arrange artichoke hearts in baking dish. If halves are used, place cut sides down. If fresh mushrooms are used, saute in butter or oil. Add mushrooms, peas, and seasonings to artichokes. Add

1-1/2 cups medium cream
   sauce
1/4 cup cracker crumbs

cream sauce. Top with crumbs. Bake in slow oven (325°) for 20 minutes.

Serves 4-6.

CREAMED HEARTS

1   package frozen artichoke hearts (cut in halves or quarters)
1-1/2 cups whipping cream
   Salt and pepper
1   tsp. lemon juice, more if needed
2 tbsp. minced parsley

While the artichoke hearts are cooking as directed on package, boil the cream in a small saucepan until it has reduced by half. Season to taste with salt, pepper, and lemon juice. When the artichokes are done, fold the hot cream into them. Simmer for a moment on top of the stove to blend flavors. Turn into a hot vegetable dish and sprinkle with parsley. Serve creamed artichoke hearts with roast veal or chicken. They also go well as a filling for omelettes.

Serves 4.

ALCACHOFA A LA MARIA

1   tbsp. minced onion
1/3 cup olive oil
1   tbsp. flour
1   cup boiling water
2   carrots, sliced
1   bunch fresh green onions, chopped
1   tsp. peppercorns
1   tsp. salt
1   tsp. dill weed
2   packages frozen artichoke hearts
   Juice of 1/2 lemon

Saute minced onion in oil. Add flour, water, carrots and green onions. Cook for 10 to 15 minutes. Add spices, artichokes and lemon juice. Cook for 45 minutes or until vegetables are tender but not watery.

Serves 6.

ALCACHOFA PORTUGUESE

1   package frozen artichoke hearts
1   medium-sized onion, chopped

Heat oil in frying pan, add onion and garlic, and cook until soft. Thaw artichokes and add to pan; cook, stirring, until lightly

2   whole cloves garlic
6   tbsp. canned tomato sauce
3/4 cup water
    Salt
2   tbsp. olive oil

browned. Mix in tomato sauce and water. Cover and simmer for 10 to 20 minutes or until artichokes are tender. Discard garlic. Salt to taste. Serve as a vegetable with any meat dish.

Serves 4.

ARTICHOKE DELIGHT

4   medium-sized artichokes
2   tbsp. butter
1   tbsp. lemon juice
1/2 lb. fresh mushrooms
1   tbsp. flour
3/4 tsp. salt
1/8 tsp. pepper
1   tbsp. chopped parsley
1/2 cup milk
1   cup heavy cream

Prepare artichokes according to Method 4 and keep them hot. Melt butter in a saucepan; add lemon juice and mushrooms, sliced. Cook until mushrooms are tender, stirring frequently. Reserve a few of these mushroom slices for garnish. Stir flour, salt, pepper and chopped parsley into mushrooms, and mix well. Gradually stir in milk and heavy cream, blending until smooth. Cook, stirring constantly, until sauce thickens. Pour sauce into hot cooked artichokes. Add mushrooms slices and a little parsley to garnish.

Serves 4.

SAUTEED ARTICHOKES

6   medium artichokes
6   tbsp. butter or margarine
1/2 tsp. basil

Prepare artichokes according to Method 2. Cut into quarters. Cool, cover; chill. Melt butter in a frying pan (or an electric frying pan) and add the artichokes and basil. Saute over medium-high heat, turning occasionally with a spatula, until portions of the artichoke are lightly browned; about 10 minutes.

Serves 6.

CELERY AND ARTICHOKES

3   large stalks celery
6   small artichokes

Prepare artichokes according to Method 2. Wash celery and cut

Salt and pepper
1/2 clove garlic
2 tbsp. olive oil
1 small onion
1 small tomato
1 tsp. minced thyme or
1/2 tsp. rosemary

into 1-inch pieces. Halve the artichokes. Cover vegetables with boiling water, add salt and pepper to taste and cook until tender. Drain. Brown halved garlic clove in oil, then add minced onion and cook slowly 10 minutes. Peel tomato and cut it up into small pieces and add to onion. Add vegetables and herbs and stir well; discard garlic, and cook slowly, covered, for 10 minutes.
Serves 4.

FONDS D'ARTICHAUTS AUX EPINARDS

4 artichoke bottoms, cooked
2 tbsp. butter
1/2 lb. spinach
3 tbsp. heavy cream
1/2 cup grated Gruyere cheese
Salt and pepper

Prepare artichokes according to Method 5. Saute the bottoms lightly in butter. Cook the spinach until tender. Then force through a strainer, food mill, or puree in a blender. Add the cream, salt and pepper. Fill each artichoke bottom with spinach. Sprinkle with grated cheese. Dot each one with butter and brown in a moderate oven (350°).
Serves 2.

FARCIS AUX CHAMPIGNONS

8 artichoke bottoms, cooked
3 tbsp. butter
1/2 lb. mushrooms
3/4 cup thick Bechamel sauce
1/4 cup grated Gruyere cheese
Salt and pepper

Prepare artichokes according to Method 5. Saute bottoms in butter. Remove to a fire-proof serving platter. Wash and trim the mushrooms. Slice them thin and saute them a few minutes in butter. Make the Bechamel sauce and and mix it into the mushrooms. Season with salt and pepper. Fill the bottoms with the mixture. Sprinkle with the grated cheese, dot with butter, and brown in a 400°F. oven for 5 to 10 minutes.
Serves 4.

ARTICHOKES A LA PROVENCALE

8 medium artichokes
8 cloves garlic
   Vinegar
3/4 cup olive oil
   Bouquet garni (bay leaf, thyme, parsley)
   Salt and pepper

Prepare artichokes according to Method 1. Place them in a shallow pan just large enough to hold the artichokes. They should be pressed one against the other. Insert the garlic between the artichokes. Pour a little vinegar into each artichoke, allowing about 1/4 teaspoon to each one. Pour the oil in the pan and then fill with water. Sprinkle with salt and pepper and add the bouquet garni. Cover and simmer 45 minutes. 15 minutes before the end of cooking, remove the cover and let the liquid boil away so that the artichokes brown slightly on the bottom.

Serves 4.

ARTICHOKES WITH MUSHROOMS

3/4 lb. mushroom halves
4 tbsp. butter
2 packages frozen artichoke hearts (thawed)
1/3 cup heavy cream
1/2 tsp. tarragon
   Salt and pepper

Cover and cook mushroom halves in butter for 5 minutes. Add thawed artichoke hearts. Cover and simmer 7 or 8 minutes longer. Stir in tarragon, and cream, and season to taste with salt and pepper.

Serves 4-6.

ARTICHOKE HEARTS AND PECANS

2 packages frozen artichoke hearts, thawed
1 cup sweet cream
2 tbsp. butter
2 tbsp. flour
   Salt and pepper to taste
   Tabasco sauce to taste
1/2 cup broken pecans
1/4 cup bread crumbs
2 tbsp. Parmesan cheese

Place artichoke hearts in small casserole. Blend cream, butter and flour; cook until thickened, stirring constantly. Season with salt, pepper and Tabasco sauce. Pour sauce into casserole; add pecans. Sprinkle with bread crumbs and cheese. Bake at 300° until bubbly.

Serves 6.

CARROT AND ONION FILLING

6 medium artichokes
2 parts white wine
1 part water
1/2 tsp. salt
1 cup carrots, diced and
    cooked
1 cup pearl onions

Prepare artichokes according to Method 3. Fill saucepan to a depth of 1/2 to 1 inch with a mixture of white wine and water; add salt. Bring liquid to a boil; add artichokes, cover and cook until just tender, about 30 minutes. Drain. Fill artichokes with carrots and onions. Arrange cups around double pork loin roast and serve hot.

Serves 6.

CARCIOFINI ALLA ROMANA

4 medium size artichokes
1/3 cup olive oil
1/4 cup water
4 cloves garlic, crushed
    Salt and pepper
1 tsp. mint flakes (or sprig of
    mint leaves)

Prepare artichokes according to Method 2. Cut into quarters and remove choke. Place them in saucepan with oil, water, mint and garlic. Sprinkle with salt and pepper, cover and let steam slowly until tender. Serve on side dish, pouring over them some of the oil in which they have been cooked.

Serves 4.

ARTICHOKES FLORENTINE

6 artichoke bottoms, cooked
1/2 lb. spinach, cooked,
    chopped and seasoned
1 cup Sauce Mornay
1/8 cup Parmesan cheese,
    grated

Prepare artichokes according to Method 5. Arrange bottoms in a shallow baking dish. Fill with spinach, cover with Sauce Mornay, sprinkle with grated Parmesan cheese, and bake in a moderately hot oven (375°) until brown.

Sauce Mornay:
1/2 cup medium or thin cream
    sauce
1 tbsp. each grated Gruyere
    or Swiss cheese and Par-
    mesan cheese
    Dash of liquid hot-pepper
    seasoning

Sauce Mornay: Make cream sauce and add grated Gruyere or Swiss cheese and Parmesan cheese. When melted, correct seasoning, add a dash of liquid hot-pepper seasoning.

For a special treat, serve this with roast leg of lamb.

Serves 6.

PARSLEY STUFFING

1   cup finely chopped parsley
1/2 cup grated Parmesan
    cheese
6   pitted ripe olives, chopped
2   small garlic cloves, minced
    or mashed
2   tsp. olive oil
    Salt and pepper
4   medium sized artichokes
1/3 cup water
1/4 cup olive oil
4   tbsp. butter or margarine

Prepare artichokes according to Method 1. Turn artichoke upside down and press down firmly to force leaves to spread apart. Remove choke. Combine parsley, cheese, olives, garlic, 2 tsp. olive oil, salt and pepper. Line the inside of each leaf with stuffing. Combine water and 1/4 cup olive oil in a saucepan; stand stuffed artichokes in pan, and top each with butter. Cover the pan and cook gently for 1 hour. Serve while hot. The cooking liquid may be used as a sauce in which to dip the artichoke leaves.

Serves 4.

BUTTERED HEARTS

1   package frozen artichoke
    hearts (cut in half or
    quarters)
4   tbsp. butter
    A 6-cup enameled
    casserole
2   tbsp. minced shallots or
    green onions
    Salt and pepper
2   tbsp. minced parsley

Cook artichokes as directed on package. Melt the butter in the casserole. Stir in the shallots or onions, then fold in the artichokes. Season with salt and pepper, and lay over them a round of buttered wax paper. Cover the casserole and bake at 325°F. for about 20 minutes, or until the vegetables are well steeped in the butter. Do not overcook. Sprinkle with parsley before serving.

Serves 4.

ARTICHOKES WITH PARSLEY SAUCE

2   packages frozen artichoke
    hearts
3   tbsp. butter
3   tbsp. flour
2   cups milk
1/2 tsp. salt
1/8 tsp. pepper
2   tbsp. minced parsley or
    parsley flakes

Cook frozen artichokes according to package directions. Drain; cut in quarters. Melt butter; stir in flour. Add milk gradually; cook until thickened, stirring constantly. Add salt and pepper; fold in minced parsley. Combine with artichokes; heat through. Sprinkle with paprika.

Serves 8.

SPINACH STUFFED

6   artichoke bottoms
     Tarragon vinegar or
     lemon juice
     Swiss cheese
     Black olives, sliced

Spinach Filling:

3   cups finely chopped
     cooked spinach
1/2 cup melted butter
1   tsp. minced shallots or
     1/3 tsp. garlic puree
1   tsp. sweet basil
1   cup flour
1/8 tsp. nutmeg
1/2 cup Sherry
1   cup scalded milk
1   tsp. monosodium
     glutamate
1/2 cup grated Parmesan
     cheese
3   eggs
     Salt and pepper to taste

Prepare artichokes according to Method 5. Cook until tender in water seasoned with tarragon vinegar or lemon juice. Remove from water, drain; season with salt and pepper.

Spinach Filling: Lightly brown the shallots in the butter, then slowly add flour and stir to a smooth paste. Sprinkle in sweet basil and nutmeg. Pour in scalded milk a little at a time, stirring constantly until smooth. Add Sherry, keep over low heat and stir until smooth and thick. Add chopped spinach and monosodium glutamate. Using a heavy spooon stir the mixture until smooth. The mixture should have a heavy consistency. Cool. Now add slightly beaten eggs and the grated Parmesan cheese. Beat again until smooth. Add salt and pepper to taste. Spoon spinach filling on prepared artichoke bottoms, round up filling to a dome-shaped top. Garnish with four strips of Swiss cheese. Place them in a cross-like fashion. Arrange a slice of black olive on top. Bake in a 350° oven for 25 minutes until thoroughly heated and cheese is melted.

Serves 6.

PEAS WITH ONIONS

1   package frozen peas and
     onions
8   artichoke bottoms
     (bottled or frozen)
1/4 tsp. butter or margarine
     Paprika

Cook frozen peas and onions as package directs. Drain artichoke bottoms. Put butter or margarine on each artichoke and arrange in a shallow pan; heat in the oven about 5 to 10 minutes. To serve, spoon hot peas and onions into the artichokes and sprinkle with paprika. Arrange two on each plate. Serves 4.

ALCACHOFA CACEROLA

3 large artichokes
1/2 tsp. salt
1 large garlic clove, sliced
1 can (10-1/2 oz.) cream of mushroom soup
1 cup half-and-half (half milk and half cream)
1/2 tsp. prepared mustard
Dash of cayenne
1/2 tsp. Worcestershire
Salt to taste
Pepper to taste
1 cup (1/4 lb.) shredded mild cheddar cheese

Cut off top 1/3 and pre-cook artichokes as in Method 1. Cut in half lengthwise; remove choke, pull off any inedible leaves. Combine soup, half-and-half, mustard, cayenne, Worcestershire, salt and pepper. Arrange artichokes in a greased 1-1/2 quart casserole; pour sauce over, and sprinkle shredded cheese over the top. Bake in a moderate oven (350°) for 30 minutes.

Serves 6.

SPINACH-ARTICHOKE CASSEROLE

3 packages frozen chopped spinach
1/2 green pepper, chopped
1 can cream of celery soup
2 slices bread
1/4 cup milk
2 eggs, beaten
Salt and pepper
Onion salt
2 packages frozen artichoke hearts
Parmesan cheese
Butter

Cook spinach according to package directions, add green pepper; drain. Add soup. Soak bread in milk; add to spinach. Add eggs and seasonings. Line the bottom of a greased casserole with artichoke hearts. Place a layer of spinach mixture on artichokes; add a thick layer of Parmesan cheese. Repeat spinach and cheese layers; dot with butter. Bake at 350° for 30 to 40 minutes.

Serves 10-12.

ARTICHOKES IN BOUILLON

6 medium-size artichokes
1 medium-size onion, chopped
1 large clove garlic, minced
1 tbsp. salad oil

Prepare artichokes according to Method 1. In a deep saucepan cook onion and garlic in oil until limp. Add bouillon, lemon juice, oregano, and salt; bring to a boil.

1   cup bouillon
2   tbsp. lemon juice
1   tps. oregano
1   tsp. salt
1   tbsp. chopped parsley

Place artichokes stem end down in broth. Baste with broth and cover tightly. Cook until tender, about 20 minutes, basting twice more. Test with fork for doneness. The time will vary with the size of the artichokes. Remove from broth, sprinkle with parsley, and serve with fish, meat, or game.

Serves 6.

TRES LEGUMBRES-EN VINO

2   packages frozen artichoke hearts
6   medium-sized new potatoes
1/2 lb. green peas
2   tbsp. olive oil
2   tbsp. butter
2   cloves garlic
1   tomato
1/4 cup dry white wine
6   leaves sweet basil
    Salt and pepper

Scrape potatoes and slice into 1/4 inch slices. Shell peas. Heat oil and butter in a skillet or casserole and to it add the garlic cloves halved lengthwise and speared with toothpicks. Brown garlic slowly, then add artichokes and potatoes, stir well, and cook 5 minutes. Add peas and the tomato which has been peeled and cut up. Stir again, add rest of ingredients. Mix well, cover, and cook slowly until potatoes and artichokes are tender. If necessary to prevent scorching, add a very little hot water from time to time. When ready to serve, all moisture should have been cooked up. Discard garlic before serving, and add more salt if necessary.

Serves 6.

MUSHROOM-STUFFED ARTICHOKE

1/4 cup (1/2 cube) butter or margarine
1/4 cup dry white wine
1/2 tsp. salt
1/4 tsp. monosodium glutamate
    Dash of freshly ground pepper

Prepare artichokes according to Method 4. Keep them warm. In a large frying pan, melt butter and add wine, salt, monosodium glutamate, and pepper. Add mushroom caps and simmer just until tender, stirring constantly. Stir sour cream into the mushrooms and

1   lb. small mushroom caps
10   large artichokes
3   tbsp. water
1/2 cup thick cultured sour
     cream
     Watercress sprigs for
     garnish

sauce, heat just until cream and sauce are blended. Spoon 3 or 4 mushrooms, along with sour cream sauce into each artichoke shell. Serve hot, as an appetizer or first course, or vegetable with a garnish of watercress.

Serves 10.

ARTICHOKE AND MUSHROOM CASSEROLE

1/2 cup butter
1   lb. mushrooms, sliced
1   medium onion, sliced
1/4 cup flour
2   cups milk
1   cup light cream
3/4 lb. sharp Cheddar cheese,
     grated
1/8 tsp. hot pepper sauce
2   tsp. soy sauce
1   tsp. salt
1/2 tsp. monosodium
     glutamate
2   packages frozen artichoke
     hearts
1   (5 oz.) can water chestnuts,
     drained and sliced
1/2 to 3/4 cup toasted, slivered
     almonds, blanched
1   package frozen green
     beans

Saute mushrooms and onion in butter. Add flour and cook until smooth. Transfer to double boiler. Add milk and cream. Stir over boiling water until thickened. Add cheese, hot pepper sauce, soy sauce, salt, pepper, and monosodium glutamate. Stir until cheese is melted. Cook green beans until just tender. Drain. Mix with the mushroom sauce and water chestnuts. Pour into a casserole and sprinkle with almonds. Bake in a 375° oven for 20 minutes, or until bubbly. If casserole has been prepared ahead and becomes cool, allow 35-40 minutes to heat thoroughly.

Serves 8-10.

ARTICHOKE FRITATA II

2   cups artichoke hearts, cut
     fine, cooked
1/2 cup milk
1/2 cup Melba crumbs
1   medium onion, sauteed in
     1 tbsp. oil
1   large clove garlic, put
     through press
2   tbsp. minced parsley
1/2 tsp. thyme

Pour milk over crumbs to moisten. Add sauteed onion. Then add remaining ingredients as given. Oil a glass baking dish with 1 tbsp. oil. Add ingredients and bake at 350° until set and browned on top, about 25 minutes. This is also good served cold in small cubes as an appetizer.

Serves 4.

Salt and pepper
1 tsp. accent
1/2 cup grated Parmesan
    cheese
4 eggs, beaten

ARTICHOKE HEARTS SURPRISE

2 packages frozen artichoke
    hearts
1 tbsp. lemon juice
1 tbsp. butter
1/4 tsp. salt
1/8 tsp. pepper
1 package frozen chopped
    broccoli
1 onion, diced
1 cup white sauce
2 tbsp. Parmesan cheese

Prepare a 1-quart shallow casserole. Preheat oven to 375°F. Cook artichoke hearts (not quite done). Drain, season with lemon juice, butter, salt and pepper. Place in casserole. Cook broccoli with onion. When finished, drain and put into blender or through food mill. Combine broccoli with white sauce and cheese. Season to taste. Spread broccoli puree completely over artichoke hearts. Bake for 10 minutes at 375°F. This unusual vegetable combination can be completely prepared the day before. Place it in the oven 10 minutes before serving. If it comes directly from refrigerator, add 5 minutes.

Serves 6.

CARCIOFINI ITALIANA

1 package frozen artichoke
    hearts
1 medium onion
1 tbsp. oil
1 cup canned tomatoes
    Salt and pepper

Chop onion and cook slowly in butter or oil until tender. Add tomatoes and artichoke hearts and season to taste. Cover and simmer 15 to 20 minutes, or until tender.

Serves 4.

ARTICHOKE HEARTS SUPREME

1 jar marinated artichoke
    hearts
3 tbsp. butter
3 tbsp. flour
1/2 cup white cooking wine

Melt butter in a 2-quart chafing dish, or electric skillet. Add flour. Blend in wine and oil from artichoke hearts. Stir until mixture begins to thicken. Slowly add milk

1   cup milk
8 to 10 tbsp. sour cream
1   tbsp. minced green onion
6   large mushrooms, sliced
3   hard-boiled eggs, quartered
    Salt and pepper to taste
1/4 tsp. paprika

and cook until thick, stirring constantly. Add sour cream, salt and pepper. When cream has dissolved, add onions, mushrooms and artichoke hearts. Top with quartered eggs. Sprinkle with paprika for garnish. Cover and continue to cook until all ingredients are hot. Serve on toast points, steamed rice or your favorite pasta, or over asparagus spears. Serves 4.

VEGETABLE DELIGHT

1   jar marinated artichoke hearts
1   package of leaf spinach
1   tbsp. butter
1/2 cup seasoned bread crumbs
1/4 cup grated Parmesan cheese
4   tbsp. chopped onion

Partially cook the spinach. (One half the recommended time.) Saute onions in butter. Combine spinach, artichoke hearts, oil, bread crumbs, onions and cheese in a casserole type dish. Bake in a 350° oven for 15 minutes. Serves 3-4.

For the Sausage Lover—Using the same recipe add crumbled fried sausage into the mixture before it is baked. Garnish with slices of hard-boiled eggs.

ARTICHOKE STUFFED MUSHROOMS

1   jar marinated artichoke hearts
6   large mushrooms at least 2-1/2 inches in diameter
2   tbsp. butter
1   green pepper, cut in pieces about 1/4 to 1/2 inch in size
1   onion, minced
1   can tuna or 1 can salad shrimp

Saute minced onion in butter. Add oil from artichoke hearts and chopped green pepper. Saute until green fades from peppers. Remove onions and peppers from skillet and set aside. Brown over medium heat, in the same skillet, the bottom sides of the mushrooms from which the stems have been removed. Place the mushrooms in a casserole dish. Fill mushrooms by first placing a layer of the seafood in the bottom of the shell, then add onion, pepper mixture, spooning any of the butter and oil that is left in the skillet over the mixture. Top each mushroom with an artichoke heart. Place casserole in a 375° oven for about 20 minutes.   Serves 4-6.

HERB STUFFED

4 medium-sized artichokes
1 small onion, minced
1 clove garlic
2 tbsp. olive oil
1 cup dry toast crumbs
1/2 tsp. minced Rosemary
1/2 tps. wild Marjoram
Dash cayenne pepper
1/2 tsp. salt
1/8 tsp. black pepper
1/4 cup hot water

A variation of this recipe is to eliminate the herbs and substitute 1 tbsp. parsley and 8 chopped anchovy fillets

Prepare artichokes according to Method 3. Cook onion and garlic in oil for 10 minutes without browning, then add all other ingredients, remove from heat and mix well. Fill casings with stuffing. then divide the remainder among them, putting it in among the leaves. Stand them up in a saucepan, pour in around them 1/2 cup boiling water in which 2 tbsp. olive oil and 2 tsp. salt have been blended. Wet a clean white cloth, lay in the saucepan over the tops of the artichokes, and tuck it in around them. Cover and cook on a slow heat for 1 hour.   Serves 4.

ALCACHOFAS CON HONGOS

1 package frozen artichoke hearts
1/3 cup olive oil
2 tbsp. minced parsley
1/2 tsp. salt
1/8 tsp. pepper
1/2 lb. mushrooms, cut in lengthwise pieces

In the bottom of a greased shallow baking dish (8″) arrange the artichoke hearts. Pour half the combined oil, parsley, salt and pepper over the hearts. Then arrange a layer of halved mushrooms, pouring the remaining oil mixture over all. Cover and bake in a moderate oven (350°) for 30 minutes.   Serves 4.

VEGETABLE MIX

1 cup cooked mushrooms, sliced
2 cups cooked artichoke

Mix mushrooms and artichoke bottoms and saute in butter until lightly browned. Add peas and

bottoms, diced
2   cups cooked or canned
      peas
1/2 cube butter

serve hot.

Serves 4-6.

SCALLOPED ARTICHOKES
1   package frozen artichoke
      hearts, cooked
2   tbsp. lemon juice
1   cup fine dry bread crumbs
      Salt and pepper
1/8 tsp. thyme
2   eggs
1   cup light cream
1   tsp. Worcestershire
      sauce

Cook artichokes according to package directions. Drain well. Place in blender at low speed for 1-2 minutes, remove from blender. Sprinkle pulp with lemon juice. Mix with crumbs. Turn into a greased baking dish and sprinkle with salt, pepper and thyme. Beat eggs and cream together, add Worcestershire sauce. Pour over artichoke pulp. Bake in a moderate oven (350°) about 30 minutes, or until set and delicately browned.

Serves 4.

Of all the artichoke dishes the flavor of those prepared with seafood is perhaps the most elegant.

CRAB CAKE SUPREME

1 jar marinated artichoke hearts
8 canned artichoke bottoms
3 cups cooked fresh, canned or frozen King crab
1-1/2 tsp. salt
1 tsp. dry mustard
1/2 tsp. pepper
1 egg yolk
2 tsp. Worcestershire sauce
1 tbsp. mayonnaise
2 tsp. snipped parsley
Cheese sauce

Combine all ingredients, except bottoms and hearts. Press or mold with hands into 8 balls. Place in refrigerator until well chilled. When well chilled, place crab ball on each artichoke bottom. Bake at 400° for 15 minutes or until thoroughly heated. Spoon on cheese sauce that has been warmed. Serve on leaf of lettuce, garnish with marinated artichoke hearts.

Serves 8.

SHRIMP-ARTICHOKE KABOBS

1 jar marinated artichoke hearts
1/3 cup lemon juice
2 cloves garlic, minced
1-1/2 tsp. salt
1/2 tsp. paprika
1/4 tsp. pepper
1 lb. raw shrimp, cleaned
Green peppers
Cherry tomatoes
Whole baby onions

Drain oil from artichoke hearts. Combine with lemon juice, garlic, salt, pepper and paprika. Pour over cleaned shrimp and refrigerate for at least 2 hours. Drain, reserving liquid for basting kabobs. On 6 greased 12 inch skewers, alternate shrimp, hearts and vegetables. Broil 3 minutes, turning once and brushing often with marinade oil. Serve with lemon wedges, chili sauce and additional artichoke hearts.

Serves 6.

ARTICHOKES VERONIQUE

6 large artichokes
1/2 cup butter or margarine
1/4 cup finely chopped onion
1/3 cup flour
1-1/2 tsp. salt
1 tsp. monosodium glutamate
1/8 tsp. black pepper
1/8 tsp. dry mustard
1/8 tsp. ground nutmeg
2-1/2 cups milk
1 cup heavy cream
1 egg, slightly beaten
4 oz. process Gruyere cheese, cut in pieces
2 cups diced cooked South African rock lobster tail meat (reserve shells)
1/2 cup small grapes
1/2 cup dry white wine

Prepare artichokes according to Method 4. Heat butter or margarine in the top of a large double boiler. Add onion and cook over medium heat about 3 minutes. Stir in a mixture of the flour and next five ingredients. Heat until bubbly. Remove from heat and gradually add the milk and cream, stirring constantly until smooth. Bring to boiling; boil 1 minute, continuing to stir. Mix a small amount of the hot mixture with the egg and stir into the hot white sauce. Cook over simmering water 3 to 5 minutes, stirring occasionally. Add the cheese and stir until cheese is melted. Stir in the lobster, grapes, and wine; heat through. Place artichokes on a heated platter. Fill them with the sauce. Garnish platter with lobster shells, lemon wedges, and clusters of grapes.

Serves 6.

QUICK TUNA BAKE

1 cup uncooked macaroni
1 8-ounce can artichoke hearts
1 can mushroom soup
1/2 tsp. Worcestershire sauce
1/8 tsp. cayenne
1/8 tsp. sweet basil, well crushed, optional
1/8 tsp. garlic salt
1 7-ounce can tuna fish
2 tbsp. toasted bread crumbs

Cook macaroni in boiling salted water until just tender (about 8 minutes). Drain and turn into 1-1/2-quart casserole which has been lightly oiled or buttered. Drain liquid from artichoke hearts and combine with soup. Blend in seasonings. Add tuna to soup mixture and mix, breaking tuna if pieces are large. Cut artichoke hearts into halves or quarters and arrange on macaroni. Pour soup-tuna mixture over artichokes. Top with crumbs. Bake in moderate oven (350°) about 20 minutes. If crumbs are not brown enough, place casserole under broiler for 2 to 3 minutes.   Serves 4.

SHRIMP DIABLE

1   lb. frozen deveined shelled
     raw shrimp
2   jars artichoke hearts
1-1/2 tsp. salt
3   tbsp. butter or margarine
3   tbsp. flour
1   tbsp. prepared mustard
2   cups milk
2   tbsp. lemon juice
1-1/2 cups coarsely crumbled
     saltine crackers
6   hard-boiled eggs, shelled

Combine shrimp with 1/2 teaspoon of the salt in a large frying pan. (Set remaining salt aside for sauce). Pour about 4 cups boiling water over shrimp, heat just to boiling, then simmer 10 minutes, or until tender. Remove shrimp and drain well. Cut each in half. Melt butter in a medium-size saucepan; stir in flour, mustard and remaining teaspoon salt; cook stirring constantly just until bubbly; slowly stir in milk. Continue cooking and stirring until sauce thickens and boils 1 minute; remove from heat. Stir in lemon juice and 1 cup of the cracker crumbs. Chop 5 of the hard-boiled eggs coarsely; lightly fold eggs, shrimp, and drained artichoke hearts into hot sauce mixture. Spoon into a buttered shallow 6-cup baking dish; sprinkle evenly with remaining cracker crumbs. Bake in moderate oven (350°) 20 minutes, or until bubbly hot and crumbs are golden. Cut remaining egg into quarters lengthwise; arrange, petal fashion, on top. Garnish with several sprigs of parsley, if you wish.
           Serves 6.

CRAB-ARTICHOKE CASSEROLE

2   (7-1/2-oz.) cans crabmeat,
     drained
1/4 cup butter or margarine
1/4 cup flour
2   tsp. salt
1/8 tsp. pepper

Flake crabmeat, removing any cartilage; set aside. Melt butter in medium-size saucepan. Remove from heat; stir in flour, salt, pepper and paprika until smooth. Add onion. Gradually stir in milk, bring

1   tsp. paprika
1   tsp. instant minced onion
3-1/4 cups milk
1-1/4 cups uncooked macaroni
    shells
1   package frozen artichoke
    hearts, or 1 (8-1/2-oz.) jar
    artichoke hearts
1/3 cup California Dry Sherry
1/4 cup grated sharp Cheddar
    cheese

to boil, stirring constantly. Reduce heat; simmer 5 minutes. Remove from heat; set aside. Prepare macaroni according to package directions; drain well. Cook artichoke hearts according to package directions; drain well. Combine crabmeat, Sherry, macaroni and artichoke hearts with sauce; mix well. Turn into a 2-1/2-quart casserole. Sprinkle with grated cheese. Bake at 350° for about 20 minutes or until bubbly. This is perfect as the hot dish for a buffet supper, with green salad, French bread, and assorted cheeses.

Serves 6-8.

CHAFING DISH SCALLOPS

1/4 cup butter or margarine
3/4 cup sliced unblanched
    almonds
1   jar marinated artichokes
1-1/2 pounds scallops
1/2 cup half-and-half (half
    milk, half cream)
3   tbsp. finely chopped
    parsley
1/2 tsp. salt
1/8 tsp. oregano
    Dash pepper
2   tbsp. dry Sherry
1   tbsp. cornstarch
1-1/2 tsp. lemon juice
    Hot cooked rice

Melt butter in blazer (top) pan of chafing dish over direct heat; add almonds, and cook until lightly browned. Stir in scallops; cook, gently stirring occasionally, until scallops lose their translucent look. Blend in half-and-half, parsley, salt, oregano and pepper. Blend Sherry smoothly with cornstarch; stir into scallops, add artichokes and cook, stirring occasionally, until thickened. Blend in lemon juice. Serve over rice as a main dish.

Serves 4.

TUNA CASSEROLE

1   package frozen artichoke
    hearts or bottoms
1   can (6-1/2-7 oz.) tuna
1/4 cup butter or margarine
1-3/4 cups milk
1/8 tsp. curry powder

Place hearts or bottoms in shallow baking dish. Drain off oil and coarsely flake tuna over and between artichoke hearts. Melt butter and blend in flour. Add milk and cook, stir until thickened.

Few drops Worcestershire
sauce
1/3 cup grated American
cheese

Blend in 1 tsp. salt, curry powder,
Worcestershire sauce. Pour over
and around artichokes and tuna.
Sprinkle with cheese. Bake in
moderate oven (350°) 15 to 20
minutes until cheese is melted.
Serves 4.

ALCACHOFA Y CAMARON CACEROLA

1 package frozen artichoke
hearts
3/4 lb. cooked shrimp
1/4 lb. fresh mushrooms, sliced
2 tbsp. butter
1 tbsp. Worcestershire sauce
1/2 cup dry Sherry
1 can cream of mushroom
soup
1/4 cup grated Parmesan
cheese
1/2 tsp. salt
1/4 tsp. pepper
Paprika
Parsley

Arrange artichoke hearts in buttered baking dish. Arrange shrimp
over artichokes. Saute mushrooms in butter for 6 minutes; add
to shrimp and artichokes. Mix
Worcestershire sauce and Sherry
with soup; pour over ingredients
in baking dish. Sprinkle with
cheese, salt, pepper and paprika.
Bake at 375° for 30 to 40 minutes.
Garnish with parsley.
Serves 4-6.

ARTICHOKE AND SHRIMP STUFFED ONIONS

4 large onions
4 artichoke bottoms,
chopped
8 fresh shrimp, shelled, deveined and cut up
6 anchovy fillets, cut up
4 tbsp. butter
2 tbsp. flour
3/4 cup milk
2 egg yolks
Salt and pepper to taste
Dash of cayenne
Bread crumbs
Dots of butter

Prepare artichokes according to
Method 5. Remove skins from
onions and parboil in salted water, uncovered, for about 8 minutes. Drain and cool. Remove centers of onions, leaving a shell
thick to retain its shape. Chop a
third of the onion centers and
saute in 2 tbsp. butter, add artichoke bottoms, shrimp and anchovies. Season with salt and
pepper. Meanwhile prepare cream
sauce: melt 2 tbsp. butter, stir in
flour, add milk gradually and let
thicken, stirring constantly. Remove from heat and stir in egg
yolks, one at a time, blending well
after each addition. Season with

38

salt and pepper and a dash of cayenne. Add shrimp and artichoke mixture to cream sauce; blend well. Stuff onion shells with mixture, sprinkle with bread crumbs and place a dot of butter on each. Bake in a well-greased baking pan in a pre-heated 350° F. oven for about 30 minutes. Perfect as a hot appetizer or served with meat, fish or fowl. Serves 4.

ARTICHOKE-LOBSTER NEWBURG

3 packages frozen artichoke hearts
1 bay leaf (optional)
2 cans cream of mushroom soup
5 tbsp. chopped onion
6 tbsp. Sherry
1 tsp. salt
1/4 tsp. garlic salt
1/4 tsp. pepper
4 cups cooked lobster, cut into bite-sized pieces
1 cup grated Cheddar cheese

Cook artichoke hearts according to package directions; add bay leaf during cooking. Drain. Combine soup, onion, Sherry and seasonings; mix well. Arrange artichoke hearts and lobster in casserole. Add soup mixture; top with cheese. Bake at 400° for 15 minutes. Service with wild rice if desired.

Serves 8.

ARTICHOKE CRAB CIOPPINO

2 jars marinated artichoke hearts
4 medium-size onions, quartered
2 garlic cloves, finely chopped
4 tbsp. olive oil
Salt and pepper
1 cup boiling water
4 medium potatoes, halved or quartered
1 quart can solid pack tomatoes
1 dozen prawns, canned or fresh (cleaned)

In large kettle or Dutch oven, saute onions, garlic and parsley in oil until onions are transparent. Add salt and pepper to taste, then 1 cup of boiling water. Add potatoes and tomatoes; cook over medium heat until the potatoes are tender. Add prawns and clams; cover and continue to cook for 15 minutes. Then, add crab, artichoke hearts and Sherry; cover, and cook until the mixture is thoroughly heated. Serve in large bowls with hot French bread.

Serves 4.

1 dozen clams (fresh in shell
   or canned)
1 can King crab
1/4 cup Sherry

CREAMED TUNA WITH ARTICHOKES

1 package frozen artichoke
   hearts
1 can (7 oz.) tuna
1 can (10-1/2 oz.) condensed
   cream of celery soup
1/4 cup milk or light cream
1 pimiento, chopped
1 tbsp. Sherry
2 tbsp. grated Swiss or
   Parmesan cheese

Prepare artichoke hearts as directed on package. Arrange them in the bottom of a shallow casserole. Place the flaked tuna over the hearts. Pour the combined celery soup, milk, pimiento and Sherry over the tuna. Bake in moderate oven (350°) for 30 minutes. Serve hot on toast points.

Serves 4.

BAKED ARTICHOKE WITH CRAB MEAT

1 jar marinated artichoke
   hearts
2 tbsp. butter
2 tbsp. flour
1 cup milk
1 can King crab
2 stalks celery, chopped
1/2 cup chopped Pimiento
3 chopped hard boiled eggs
1 cup bread crumbs
   Oil from artichoke hearts

Combine butter, oil, flour and milk to form a white sauce. Add all ingredients except artichoke hearts and bread crumbs. Pour half of mixture in a buttered casserole. Arrange drained hearts on top of mixture. Pour remaining mixture over all. Sprinkle with bread crumbs and bake in a moderate oven (350°) for 35 minutes.

Serves 4-6.

ARTICHOKE BOTTOMS GOURMET

4 artichoke bottoms, cooked
   Butter
1/4 lb. fresh mushrooms,
   sliced
1/4 cup finely chopped green
   onion
1/4 lb. fresh cooked or canned
   crab meat
1/4 cup flour
1 cup chicken broth
1/2 cup light cream
   Dash tabasco and
   Worcestershire sauce

Prepare artichokes according to Method 5. Saute mushrooms and green onions in 1/4 cup butter for 2 minutes. Add crab meat and cook just long enough to heat. Keep warm. Melt 1/4 cup butter in saucepan; stir in flour. Add chicken broth and cream and cook, stirring until thickened and mixture boils. Season to taste with tabasco, Worcestershire sauce, salt and monosodium glutamate. To serve, place artichoke bottoms

Salt; monosodium
glutamate

on warm plate. Spoon crab mixture on artichokes and top with
sauce. Sprinkle with paprika.

Serves 2.

SALMON LOAF

1 jar marinated artichoke
hearts
1 can salmon
4 yolks of hard boiled eggs
2 cups milk
2 tbsp. butter
3 tbsp. flour
Salt and pepper to taste
Chopped parsley
1 raw egg beaten

Combine milk, butter, flour, salt
and pepper to form a thick white
sauce. Add flaked salmon, pieces
of marinated artichoke hearts and
crumbled egg yolks. Place mixture in buttered baking dish, brush
top with beaten egg, cover with
bread crumbs and dot with butter.
Bake at 375° for 15 minutes. Garnish with parsley before serving.

Serves 4.

CRAB CASSEROLE WITH ARTICHOKE HEARTS

3 tbsp. butter or margarine
3 tbsp. flour
1 cup milk
1/2 cup shredded medium
sharp Cheddar cheese
or Swiss cheese
2 tsp. Worcestershire
2 packages frozen artichoke
hearts
3/4 lb, crab meat
4 hard boiled eggs (sliced)
2 tbsp. Parmesan cheese
Crab legs, garnish

Melt butter or margarine in a
saucepan, mix in flour and gradually stir in milk. Cook until thickened, stirring constantly. Slowly
blend in Cheddar or Swiss cheese
and Worcestershire; cook until
cheese melts. Cook artichoke
hearts according to package directions. Drain. Spoon a little sauce
in the bottom of a 1-1/2-quart casserole. Alternate layers of cooked
and drained artichoke hearts (reserving a few of the nicest for
garnish), and egg slices and crab
meat. Make a middle layer of half
the sauce, and top casserole with
remaining sauce. Sprinkle with
Parmesan cheese. At this point
you can refrigerate the casserole
until you are ready to bake in a
moderate oven (350°) for 30 minutes. Garnish with crab legs and
artichoke hearts just before
serving.

Serves 4-5.

SHRIMP ESPANOL

1 jar marinated artichoke hearts
2 cups cooked shrimp
1/2 medium onion, chopped fine
2 stalks celery, chopped
1 8-oz. can tomato sauce
1/2 cup water
1/2 tsp. crushed oregano
2 tbsp. Spanish style tomato sauce
  Salt and pepper to taste

Drain oil from artichoke hearts. Combine with onion and celery and saute over low heat until onion and celery are clear. Add tomato sauce, water, salt, pepper, oregano and artichoke hearts. Simmer over low heat for 15 minutes, add shrimp and simmer 20 minutes longer. Serve over rice.

Serves 6.

STUFFED SICILIAN STYLE

4 large artichokes
1/2 cup olive oil
1/2 medium onion, minced
1 clove garlic, crushed
1 tbsp. chopped parsley
2 tbsp. olive oil
1 cup bread crumbs
2 tbsp. butter
4 or 5 anchovy fillets
1/4 tsp. pepper
  Olive oil

Prepare artichokes according to Method 1. Turn artichoke upside down and press down firmly to force leaves to spread apart. Remove choke. Combine butter and anchovies; and with a fork or blade of knife make a smooth paste. Place in a saucepan 1/2 cup olive oil, onion, garlic and parsley. Brown slowly until onion is golden. At the same time, brown the bread crumbs in a small frying pan with 2 tbsp. olive oil. When onion is tender, add toasted bread crumbs, anchovy paste, pepper and mix well. Stuff centers and between leaves of artichokes. Arrange artichokes standing up in a baking pan. Pour 1 cup of water into the bottom of pan and pour olive oil generously over artichokes. Cover and bake in slow oven (325°) until bottoms of artichokes are soft to the fork. Serve hot or cold on individual plates.

Serves 4.

SHRIMP CASSEROLE

2-1/2 cups sliced fresh
    mushrooms
1/4 cup butter or margarine
5   tbsp. flour
1/2 cup milk
2   cups light cream
    (or half-and-half)
1/2 tsp. each salt and
    monosodium glutamate
1   tps. Worcestershire
2   drops liquid hot-pepper
    seasoning
1   tsp. each parsley flakes
    and instant minced onions
2   packages frozen artichoke
    hearts
2   lbs. medium-sized shrimp,
    cooked, peeled, and
    deveined
1/2 cup shredded Gruyere
    cheese

Saute the mushrooms in butter for 5 minutes. Add flour and stir about 3 minutes. Remove from heat and gradually stir in the milk and light cream. Add the salt, monosodium glutamate, Worcestershire and onion; cook, stirring until thickened. Set aside. Drain the canned artichoke hearts arrange on bottom of a greased shallow casserole (about 8 by 12 inches). Arrange cooked shrimp over artichokes. Pour over the mushroom sauce and sprinkle with the cheese. Bake, uncovered, in a moderately hot oven (375°) for about 20 minutes, or until heated through. Garnish with pimiento strips and green olive slices when you serve.

Serves 8.

SHRIMP SAGANAKI

1   lb. raw medium-sized
    shrimp
1   package frozen artichoke
    hearts
4   tbsp. olive oil
1/4 lb. small whole mushrooms
2   cloves garlic, finely
    chopped
1/2 tsp. salt
    Freshly ground pepper
1/2 tsp. crumbled dried
    oregano
2   tbsp. lemon juice
2   tbsp. finely chopped
    parsley

Peel and devein shrimp. Cook artichoke hearts in boiling salted water for 2 minutes, then drain. Heat olive oil in a frying pan, add shrimp and mushrooms, and cook, stirring, until shrimp turn pink. Add artichoke hearts, garlic, salt, pepper, and oregano; heat until hot through. Sprinkle with lemon juice and stir lightly to blend flavors. Sprinkle with parsley. Place over a warmer to keep hot. Serve over rice as an entree or as an appetizer.

Serves 4.

SALMON LOAF A LA ARTICHOKE

1 jar marinated artichoke
    hearts
1   can salmon

Combine milk, butter, flour, salt and pepper to form a white sauce. When thick add flaked salmon,

43

1/2 cup bread crumbs
4 yolks of hard boiled eggs
2 cups milk
2 tbsp. butter
3 tbsp. flour
  Salt and pepper to taste
  Chopped parsley for garnish
1 whole egg

leaves of artichoke hearts, and crumbled egg yolks. Place mixture into buttered baking dish. Brush top with well beaten egg, cover with bread crumbs. Dot with butter. Bake at 375° for 15 minutes. Garnish with parsley before serving.

Serves 4.

CALIFORNIA CRAB ARTICHOKE CASSEROLE

2 jars marinated artichoke hearts
1 lb. crab meat
1/4 lb. fresh mushrooms
1 tsp. Worcestershire sauce
1/2 cup cooking Sherry
1 can chicken gravy
1/4 cup heavy cream
  Salt, cayenne, and pepper to taste
1/4 cup chopped toasted almonds
1/4 cup sliced ripe olives
1/4 cup buttered bread crumbs
1/4 cup Parmesan cheese

Drain artichokes and save oil to saute the mushrooms. Arange the artichokes in a buttered casserole dish. Sprinkle with crab. Slice and saute the mushrooms in oil and arrange these over the crab. Add Worcestershire sauce and Sherry to gravy. Add olives and nuts. Pour over the mixture. Top with cheese and buttered crumbs. Bake at 350° for 30 minutes.

Serves 5.

ARTICHOKE TOPPED SWORDFISH

1 jar marinated artichoke hearts
2 lbs. swordfish steaks
3 tbsp. lemon juice
1 tsp. salt
1/2 tsp pepper
1-1/2 cups commercial sour cream
1/2 cup fine cracker crumbs
2 tbsp. butter

Drain the oil from hearts and coat baking dish with this oil. Combine lemon juice, salt and pepper. Sprinkle over fish. Top fish with artichoke hearts. Spoon sour cream over the top of fish, top with cracker crumbs. Dot with butter. Bake in a 400° oven for 35-40 minutes.

Serves 6.

FISHERMAN STYLE

2 jars marinated artichoke hearts
1 can King Crab meat

While spaghetti is cooking, heat the artichokes and crabmeat in a saucepan. In another saucepan

1 can meatless Italian spaghetti sauce
1/4 cup butter
garlic salt to taste
enough cooked spaghetti for 6
parmesan cheese

heat spaghetti sauce. In a third saucepan melt the butter and add the garlic salt. Place the cooked spaghetti on a large platter and arrange the crab and artichokes alternately across the top. Pour spaghetti sauce over half the dish and garlic butter over the other half. Sprinkle with Parmesan cheese.

Serves 6.

OYSTER-ARTICHOKE

Makes 4 ramekins:
1-1/2 cups artichoke pulp
3 tbsp. butter
1-1/2 tbsp. flour
3/4 tsp. salt
3/4 tsp. pepper
1/4 tsp. hot sauce
2 tbsp. paprika
1/2 tsp. thyme
2 dozen oysters and oyster liquor
1 tbsp. chopped pimento
1 clove crushed garlic (optional)
3/4 cup bread or cracker crumbs
1 ounce sherry
4 ramekins (or large oyster shells)

Brown flour in butter, add seasoning, oyster water, and artichoke pulp. Broil oysters in a little butter until they curl. Mix all ingredients, adding sherry last. Place mixture in ramekins, top with crumbs and dot with butter. Sprinkle with paprika. Heat in oven, 450°, 10 minutes or until crumbs are brown. Mushrooms may be added if desired.

Serves 4.

Poultry

Chicken becomes delicately accented with the nut-like flavor of artichokes and can be served with a host of accompaniments such as savoury wild rice.

POULET ET ARTICHAUTS A LA CREME

2 packages frozen artichoke hearts
2 cups sliced chicken or 3 breasts
2 cups cream of chicken soup
1 cup mayonnaise
1 tsp. lemon juice
1/2 tsp. curry
1/2 cup shredded sharp American cheese
1/2 cup soft bread crumbs
1 tbsp. butter (melted)

Cook artichoke hearts according to package directions; drain. Arrange artichoke hearts in a greased baking dish. Place chicken on top. Combine soup, mayonnaise, lemon juice and curry powder, pour over chicken. Sprinkle with cheese. Combine bread crumbs and butter; sprinkle over all. Bake at 350° for 25 to 30 minutes.

Serves 6-8.

CHICKEN CASSEROLE

2 whole chicken breasts, split
4 each thighs and drumsticks
Salt and pepper
Flour
5 tbsp. butter or margarine
1/4 cup minced onion
1/4 cup chicken broth
3/4 cup dry white table wine
1/2 lb. mushrooms, sliced
3 tbsp. butter or margarine
1 package frozen artichoke hearts

Sprinkle chicken pieces with salt and pepper and coat lightly with flour. Heat the 5 tbsp. butter in a frying pan and quickly brown chicken on all sides. Arrange pieces closely together in a single layer in a large shallow baking pan; cook until soft. Add chicken broth and wine; bring to a boil, then pour over chicken. Bake, covered, in a moderately hot oven (375°) for 40 minutes. Meanwhile saute artichokes in the 3 tbsp. butter. When chicken has cooked for 40 minutes, add

47

the mushrooms and artichokes; continue baking, covered, for 8 minutes more, or until artichokes are just heated. Arrange on a platter or serve from a chafing dish. Serves 8.

CHICKEN DIVINE

6   chicken breasts
    Salt, pepper, onion, bay
    leaf
    Water
1   package frozen artichoke
    hearts
1   (10½ oz.) can cream of
    mushroom soup
1   (4 oz.) can mushroom
    stems and pieces
1   tsp. Worcestershire
1/4 tsp. nutmeg
1/2 cup mayonnaise
1/2 cup Sherry
1/2 cup whipped cream
    Grated Parmesan cheese

Cook chicken breasts with seasonings until tender. Remove from bone in fairly large piecs. Combine soup, mushrooms, seasonings, mayonnaise and Sherry. Mix well and fold in whipped cream. Neatly layer chicken, artichoke hearts, sauce and cheese in baking dish. Bake in 350° oven until bubbly, 45 to 60 minutes. Serves 6.

CHICKEN IN A HURRY

2   jars marinated artichoke
    hearts
1   cut-up frying chicken
1   cube butter or margarine
    Flour to dredge chicken
    Salt and pepper to taste
1/2 cup Sherry or sweet cooking wine
1   can cream of mushroom
    soup
    Rice or mashed potatoes

Combine flour, salt and pepper and dredge chicken until well covered. Melt butter in skillet and brown chicken. Cover the pieces of chicken when well browned with artichoke hearts and the oil from the jars plus wine. Simmer over low heat for 35 minutes or until tender. Add mushroom soup, turning the pieces of chicken so the sauce and soup will mix. Continue simmering until soup is well heated. Serve with fluffy rice or mashed potatoes. Serves 4.

CHICKEN ARTICHOKE CACCIATORE

1   jar marinated artichoke
    hearts
1   large frying chicken

Drain artichoke hearts, putting liquid and olive oil in a large skillet. Dredge chicken in flour

2   tbsp. olive oil
1   No. 2. can tomatoes
2   cloves garlic, minced
1-1/4 tsp. salt
1   tsp. monosodium glutamate
1/2 tsp. oregano
1/2 tsp basil
1/2 tsp. pepper
1/2 lb. fresh mushroom slices
    or 1 can mushroom pieces
1/4 cup Sherry
    Chopped parsley
    Flour

and brown in oil mixture until golden. Place in a large casserole. Add tomatoes to skillet and stir. Add garlic and all spices and mushrooms, stir well. Pour over chicken, spreading evenly. Cover and bake in a 350° oven for 1 hour or until tender. During the last few minutes of cooking, add Sherry. Serve garnished with chopped parsley.

Serves 4.

BAKED CHICKEN MARSALA
3-1/2 lb. frying chicken, dis-
    jointed
3   tbsp butter
4   small white onions
1   jar marinated artichoke
    hearts
1   firm ripe tomato
1   tbsp. shredded parsley
1/8 tsp garlic powder
2   tbsp. water
1/4 cup California Marsala or
    Sherry
1/4 cup shredded Parmesan
    cheese

Brown chicken in butter until deep golden. Remove chicken to a 2-quart casserole as browned. Peel onions and cut into chunks. Drain artichokes; cut in halves. Cut tomato into small chunks. Saute onions and artichokes in pan after chicken is browned. Add parsley, garlic powder and water. Cook, stirring constantly, until all brown clinging to pan has been dissolved. Stir in tomatoes and Marsala. Pour Marsala mixture over chicken. Cover and bake in a moderate oven (350°) 50 minutes until chicken is tender. Remove cover. Sprinkle with cheese and return to oven 5 minutes longer until cheese is melted.

Serves 4.

SHERRIED ARTICHOKE CHICKEN
1   frying chicken, about 3 lbs,
    cut in serving pieces
    salt and pepper
    Paprika
6   tbsp. butter or margarine
1   package frozen artichoke
    hearts

Sprinkle chicken generously with salt, pepper and paprika. In skillet, brown chicken pieces on all sides in 4 tbsp. butter; transfer to 2-quart casserole. Arrange artichoke hearts between chicken pieces. Add remaining butter to

1/4 lb. fresh mushrooms, sliced
3 tbsp. chopped scallions
2 tbsp. flour
2/3 cup chicken broth
1/4 cup sherry
1/2 tsp. crumbled dried rosemary

the drippings in skillet; add mushrooms and scallions and saute just until tender. Sprinkle flour over mushrooms and stir in chicken broth, sherry and rosemary. Cook, stirring a few minutes; pour over chicken. Cover and bake in moderate oven (375° F). 40 minutes, or until chicken is tender.

CHICKEN JERUSALEM
3 2-lb. chickens (cut up)
1 package frozen or 1 jar marinated artichoke hearts
1/2 lb. sliced fresh mushrooms
2 cups half & half or whipping cream
1/2 cup Sherry
1 tbsp. chicken base seasoning
Olive oil
4 tbsp. flour
1/4 nutmeg (optional)

Wash and dry chicken; roll in flour and brown in oil. Remove excess oil from frying pan, except for about 4 tbsp. To this oil, add 4 tbsp. of flour. Mix thoroughly. Add sherry, nutmeg, artichokes and mushrooms. Stir until thickened. Add chicken and simmer for 30 minutes. Heat cream and add just before serving. Serve with rice and minted peas.

Serves 6.

TARRAGON CHICKEN STUFFING
1/4 cup butter
3 tbsp. flour
1 cup light cream
1 cup chicken broth
1 tsp salt
1/2 tsp tarragon
2 cups diced cooked chicken
4 or 5 artichokes
2 tbsp. Sherry

Prepare artichokes according to Method 4. Melt butter; blend in flour; stir in light cream and chicken broth. Cook and stir over medium heat until sauce thickens and bubbles. Mix in salt, tarragon, diced cooked chicken. Fill casings with mixture and heat through. Just before serving stir in 2 tbsp. Sherry.

Serves 4.

POLLO ALLA ROMANA
3 whole chicken breasts
1/4 cup butter or margarine
1 can (3 or 4 oz.) whole mushrooms
2 medium-sized onions, thinly sliced

Remove the bones from the chicken breasts and cut the meat into bite-sized pieces; brown slowly in the butter or margarine, stirring occasionally. Drain mushrooms, reserving liquid. Add the onions,

2 packages frozen artichoke
   hearts, thawed
1/2 tsp. each thyme and sweet
   basil
   Salt and pepper to taste
1   tsp. chicken boullion

artichoke hearts, mushrooms, thyme, basil, salt, and pepper. Dissolve the boullion in the mushroom liquid (¼ to ⅓ cup in all) and pour over the ingredients in the frying pan. Cook, stirring occasionally, until the chicken and vegetables are tender, about 5 minutes. Serve on individual plates and pour parsley-sour cream sauce over each serving.
Serves 4 to 6.

Meat

BISTECCA ALCACHOFAS

1 jar marinated artichoke hearts
1-1/2 lbs. beef round steak
2 tbsp. butter or margarine
Oil from artichokes
1 cup sliced onions
1/2 cup celery, sliced diagonally
1 clove garlic, minced
2 tbsp. brown sugar
1 small can mushrooms
3/4 cup red wine or water
1 can beef consomme or 1 cup beef bouillon
1 pint sour cream
Salt and pepper to taste

Dredge beef which has been cut into strips in flour, salt and pepper. Brown beef strips in butter and oil. Add onions, celery and saute until tender. Add meat, garlic, brown sugar, wine and beef stock. Cook for 1 hour over medium heat. After mixture has cooked, add artichoke hearts and mushrooms and cook for an additional ½ hour or until the meat is tender. Just before serving add sour cream and heat to serving temperature. Serve over rice or egg noodles.

Serves 6-8.

SPARERIBS WITH ARTICHOKES

2 sides spareribs (about 4 pounds)
1/4 cup oil or fat
24 very small artichokes
2-1/2 cups cooked tomatoes (no. 2 can)
2 cloves garlic, minced
1 tsp. salt
1/2 tsp. sage
1/2 tsp rosemary

Cut spareribs into serving pieces. Brown in oil or fat. (Olive oil is usually used.) Trim and wash artichokes thoroughly. Drain well and pat dry. Arrange artichokes in and around the meat. Add tomatoes and seasonings. Cover and bake in a moderate over (350°) until meat and artichokes are tender, about 1½ hours.

Serves 6.

ALCACHOFAS ALLA VITELLO Y CAPSICAN

4 large artichokes
1/4 cup olive oil
1-1/2 lbs. veal cutlet, coarsely

Prepare artichokes according to Method 4. Heat oil; add veal. Cook over medium heat, stirring

chopped
1 large green pepper, chopped
1 medium onion, chopped
1 clove garlic, crushed
1 tsp. salt
1/4 tsp. pepper
2 medium tomatoes, chopped
1/3 cup grated Parmesan cheese

occasionally, about 10 minutes. Add green pepper, onion, garlic, salt and pepper; mix well. Cook 10 minutes, stirring occasionally Add tomatoes, cheese; mix well. Cover and cook over low heat, stirring often, 20 to 25 minutes. Turn cooked artichokes upside down and fill with veal mixture.
Serves 4.

TOURNEDOS ROYAL
4 artichokes
1/4 cup butter
1/2 cup chopped onion
1/4 cup bread crumbs
1 tsp. paprika
1 tsp. capers
1 tsp. chopped truffles
Pinch powdered thyme
1 cup sweetbreads, parboiled and chopped fine
4 fillets mignon (12 to 14 ounces each)
1/4 cup Bearnaise Sauce

Prepare artichokes according to Method 4. Cut off ⅔ and discard. In a small skillet melt butter and saute onion, bread crumbs, paprika, capers, truffles and thyme until done. Add sweetbreads and heat through. Remove pan from heat. Divide mixture in 4 portions and roll into balls. Place each ball in an artichoke cup. Season fillets and grill to taste. Place each fillet on a serving plate. Pour about 1 tbsp. Bearnaise sauce over each fillet and place stuffed artichoke cup on top.
Serves 4.

BEEF STUFFED
6 large artichokes
1/2 lb. ground lean beef
1/2 cup chopped onion
Oil
2 tbsp. chopped parsley
3/4 cup soft bread crumbs
1 egg
Salt and pepper to taste
1 tomato
2 tbsp. lemon juice

Prepare artichokes according to Method 3. Brown beef and onion in about 2 tbsp. olive oil or other cooking oil. Remove from heat, stir in parsley and fill centers of artichokes with meat mixture. Place artichokes in deep baking dish; top each with thin slice of tomato. Put one inch boiling water in baking pan; add lemon juice, top generously with salt and pepper; cover. Bake in moderate oven (350°) about 1½ hours or until tender.
Serves 6.

WITH SALAMI

12 small artichokes
3 tbsp soft butter
2 tbsp. each fine soft bread crumbs, grated dry jack cheese, and finely minced Italian dry salami
1 tbsp. finey chopped parsley
1 clove garlic, minced or mashed

Prepare artichokes according to Method 1. Turn artichokes upside down and press down firmly to force leaves to spread apart. Remove choke. Make a paste by creaming together the butter, bread crumbs, cheese, salami, parsley, and garlic. Spoon about 1 tsp. of the paste on top of each artichoke; pressing it down between the leaves. Stand artichokes in 1-inch of water in a large kettle or steamer; cover. Steam about 35 minutes, until artichokes are tender.

Serves 6.

ARTICHOKES SAUTEED WITH HAM

1 package frozen artichoke hearts
1/2 cup boiling water
1 lemon slice
1/2 tsp. salt
1/3 to 1/2 cup ham, cut in slivers
2 tbsp. butter or olive oil
1 tbsp. chopped green onion
1 tsp. finely chopped parsley
1 small clove garlic, minced or mashed

Add the artichokes to the boiling water along with the lemon and salt. Cook until just tender—be careful not to overcook them. Meanwhile lightly brown the ham in the butter or olive oil in a frying pan. Add the onion, parsley, and garlic; cover the pan and cook about 5 minutes. Add the drained artichoke hearts and heat, stirring gently.

Serves 2 to 3.

HAM AND ARTICHOKE CASSEROLE

2 packages frozen artichoke hearts
1 bay leaf (optional)
2 cans cream of mushroom soup
1 tsp. onion, chopped
1/4 cup Sherry
1/4 tsp. garlic salt
1/2 tsp. salt
Pepper to taste
2 cups diced cooked ham

Cook artichokes with bay leaf as directed on package. Drain and remove bay leaf. Combine soup, onion, Sherry, Garlic salt, salt and pepper; mix well. Arrange artichoke hearts, ham and eggs in 3-quart casserole. Pour soup mixture over all; top with cheese slices. Bake at 400° for 25 to 30 minutes.

Serves 8.

8 hard - boiled eggs, quartered

4 slices American cheese

VITELLO AL CARCIOFINI

2 cloves garlic
  Oil (half olive oil, if preferred)
2 lbs. veal round (have butcher flatten to ¼ in)
  Flour seasoned with salt and pepper
1 (1-lb.) can solid-pack tomatoes
1/2 cup Sherry or Sauterne
1/4 tsp. oregano
2 packages frozen artichoke hearts

In a heavy skillet, saute garlic in oil. Dust veal with seasoned flour; brown in oil. Add tomatoes, wine and oregano; mix well. Add frozen artichoke hearts. Cover; simmer 45 minutes to 1 hour, or until meat is tender. Serve with steamed rice, tossed green salad, french bread and fresh fruit dessert.

Serves 6.

STUFFED ARTICHOKES—HAM AND RICE

4 artichokes
1 cup diced cooked ham
1 cup cooked rice
2 tbsp. dry Sherry
1 small tomato, diced
2 tbsp. melted butter
1/4 cup grated Parmesan cheese
1/2 tsp. seasoned salt

Prepare artichokes according to Method 3. Combine cooked ham and rice, dry Sherry, tomato, melted butter, Parmesan cheese, and seasoned salt. Fill the cooked artichokes with the ham and rice mixture. Arrange the stuffed artichokes in a 2-quart casserole, cover and bake at 350° for 15 to 20 minutes.   Serves 4.

SYRIAN ARTICHOKES

6 large artichokes
1-1/2 lb. lamb
2 medium size onions
  Salad oil
1/2 cup celery, sliced
1 tsp. salt
1/4 tsp. ground cumin
1/4 tsp. curry powder
1/4 tsp. pepper
1/8 tsp. cinnamon
1/8 tsp. allspice
1 can (8-oz.) tomato sauce

Prepare artichokes according to Method 3. Cut lamb in ½-inch cubes or smaller and saute with coarsely chopped onions in a small amount of salad oil in a large frying pan until onions are translucent. Add sliced celery; continue cooking about 5 minutes. Season mixture with salt, ground cumin, curry powder, pepper, cinnamon and allspice. Combine tomato sauce, tomato paste,

1 can (6-oz.) tomato paste
3/4 cup pineapple juice
2 tsp. sugar
1 tsp. soy sauce
1 tsp. Worcestershire

pineapple juice, sugar, soy sauce and Worcestershire; measure out ¾ cup and reserve. Pour remainder over meat mixture and mix well; then spoon into the artichokes and place them in a large greased baking pan. Pour remaining sauce over each. Bake in a moderately slow oven (325°) for 1 hour.   Serves 6.

LAMB-WHEAT STUFFED ARTICHOKES

4 artichokes
1 cup boiling water
1/2 cup cracked wheat (bulgar)
1 lb. ground lamb
2/3 cup chopped onion
1 clove garlic, halved
1/3 cup pine nuts
1/4 cup butter
2 tsp. chopped fresh mint
1-1/4 tsp. salt
1/2. tsp ground thyme
1/4 tsp. pepper
2 tbsp. Worcestershire
2 ounces rose wine

Prepare artichokes according to Method 4. Pour boiling water over cracked wheat in a bowl. Let stand 30 minutes; drain. Combine wheat, lamb, and ⅓ cup onion; put through food grinder. In a saucepan, saute ⅓ cup onion, garlic clove, and pine nuts in butter for 2 minutes. Add the lamb mixture, chopped fresh mint, salt, ground thyme, pepper and Worcestershire. Brown over medium heat, stirring constantly. Finally, stir in rose wine. Fill the hot artichokes with the mixture. Garnish with parsley and serve with melted butter, if desired.
                    Serves 4.

SAUSAGE STUFFED

4 large artichokes
1 lb. sweet Italian sausages, casings removed
1/2 cup dried mushrooms
1 egg
2 tbsp. grated Parmesan cheese
1 tbsp. chopped parsley
Salt and pepper
Bread crumbs
Butter
1 tbsp. tomato paste, dissolved

Prepare artichokes according to Method 4. Soak mushrooms in a little warm water until softened; drain and chop. Prepare dressing: crumble sausage meat and saute in a little butter until almost done; remove from heat. Add chopped mushrooms, the whole egg, grated cheese, parsley; mix and blend well, seasoning with salt and pepper to taste. Stuff artichoke centers with this dressing

57

in 1 cup water

and push some down between the leaves. Sprinkle tops with bread crumbs, dot with butter and arrange them upright in a baking dish. Pour the dissolved tomato paste in the bottom of baking dish and bake in a preheated 375° oven for about 30 to 45 minutes, basting occasionally.   Serves 4.

YAHNIT EL ARDISHAWKI
8   medium artichokes
2   lbs. boneless lamb
1/4 cup flour
2   tsp. salt
1/4 tsp. pepper
1/4 cup salad oil
1-1/2 cup chopped onion
1   tbsp. flour
4   cups water
1   tsp. salt
     Dash ground pepper

Prepare artichokes according to Method 2. Cut into quarters. Cut lamb in cubes, roll in flour, seasoned with salt and pepper. Heat oil in a Dutch oven or large heavy frying pan; saute the meat until brown on all sides. Add onions and when lightly browned, sprinkle with flour; stir until blended. Add 4 cups water. Cover the pan and cook 20 minutes; add salt, some freshly ground pepper, and the drained artichoke hearts. Cover and cook until tender, about 40 minutes, adding more salt and lemon juice to taste. Serve with hot cooked rice.   Serves 8.

LAMB LEBANESE
1-1/2 lb. lamb cut in ½-inch
     cubes
1   large onion, coarsely
     chopped
3   small tomatoes, diced
1/3 cup pine nuts
1   tsp. monosodium glutamate
1/2 tsp. pepper
1/8 tsp. cinnamon
1   tsp. salt
1   package frozen artichoke
     hearts
1   can (8-oz.) tomato sauce
1/2 tsp. salt

Mix together lamb cubes, chopped onion, tomatoes, pine nuts, monosodium glutamate, pepper, cinnamon, and salt. Spoon this mixture into a buttered 2-quart casserole. Lightly saute artichoke hearts in butter, then arrange over the mixture. Season tomato sauce with salt, and pour it over artichoke hearts. Bake uncovered, in a moderately slow oven (325°) for 2 hours.

Serve this casserole with rice, a green salad dressed with oil and vinegar. If you can't get pine nuts, substitute sliced almonds.

Serves 4.

CROQUETTES DE MOUTON AUX ARTICHAUTS

4 artichoke bottoms
1-1/2 cups leftover lamb
1-1/2 cups thick Bechamel
   sauce
2 eggs
   Pinch of nutmeg
   Soft bread crumbs
   Juice of 1 lemon
1 cup heavy cream
   Salt and pepper

Prepare artichokes according to Method 5. Cut the artichoke bottoms into small dice. Chop rather coarsely or dice the leftover lamb, which should be free from all gristle. Make the Bechamel sauce and add the artichokes, lamb, 2 egg yolks, nutmeg, salt, and pepper. Mix it well and spread it out on a cookie sheet or other working surface to cool. When cold, make small balls of this mixture. Dip each one into egg white, which has been beaten to a froth, and then into the bread crumbs. Fry the balls in deep fat (385°) F. until golden brown. At the same time, heat the cream without boiling and season it lightly with salt, pepper and lemon juice. Drain the croquettes on paper toweling and serve hot accompanied by the hot cream.

Serves 4.

VEAL WITH ARTICHOKES

1 package frozen artichoke
   hearts
4 veal steaks
1/2 tsp. salt
1/4 tsp. garlic salt
1 lemon
1/4 cup dry white wine or
   Vermouth
1 tbsp. butter

Place frozen artichoke hearts in boiling water; simmer 3 minutes and drain. Quickly saute veal steaks in the butter; turn to brown on both sides. Season with salt and garlic salt and remove to a hot platter. Add drained artichoke hearts to pan drippings and heat just until lightly browned; spoon along one side of the veal steaks. Halve lemon lengthwise; cut one half into 4 wedges to garnish platter; squeeze juice from other half into pan. Pour wine or Vermouth into pan and let cook down until reduced one-half. Spoon over veal. Garnish with lemon wedges.

Serves 4.

CARCIOFI VIGNAROLA

4 large artichokes
2 tbsp. butter
1 head lettuce, shredded
20 strips of bacon, chopped
1 lb. fresh peas
1/2 head fennel
1 sliced carrot
8 small new potatoes
1 large tomato
2 cups water
1 cup dry white wine
2 tsp. salt
1/4 tsp. pepper
1 Celery heart, chopped

Prepare artichokes according to Method 3. Grease a casserole large enough to hold the artichokes with butter. Shred lettuce and spread it on bottom of casserole. Chop bacon and sprinkle pieces on top of lettuce. Place artichokes on the bed of lettuce. Shell peas and fill centers of artichokes with them. Surround artichokes with hearts of celery, chopped fennel, sliced carrots, new potatoes peeled, and tomato, cut in wedges. Add water, wine salt and pepper. Bring liquid to a simmer, cover casserole tightly, and cook over low heat for 1¼ hours.

Serves 4.

ALCACHOFAS RELLENAS

4 Large artichokes

Prepare artichokes according to Method 3. Then take some garlic sausage, chop up very fine with some onions and parsley, and force this between the leaves of the artichokes. Bake in a pan containing plenty of olive oil, in a moderate oven (350°) about 30 minutes, or until tender. Keep basting them with the oil.

Marinated artichoke hearts are wonderful no matter how you serve them. They seem to appear most often as appetizers or in salads. But they make a great addition to any number of prepared dishes.

MRS. CESCHI'S PICKLED ARTICHOKES

2 dozen tiny artichokes
3 cloves garlic, sliced very thin
1 tbsp. chopped parsley
1 tbsp. chopped onion
2 medium green peppers, chopped
  Juice of 1 lemon (about 3 tbsp.)
1/4 cup olive oil
1/4 cup wine vinegar

Prepare artichokes according to Method 2. Drain well. Put artichokes in a bowl, add the chopped vegetables and stir gently until the artichokes are well coated. Slowly add the lemon juice, olive oil, and vinegar, stirring gently with each addition. Use within a few days. Refrigerate until used.

"QUICKIE" MARINATED ARTICHOKE HEARTS

1 package frozen artichoke hearts
2 tbsp. lemon juice
2 tbsp. olive oil
1 clove garlic, crushed
1/4 tsp. salt
  Dash pepper
  Dash paprika
  Lemon slices

Cook artichoke hearts according to package directions; drain. Mix lemon juice, olive oil, garlic, salt, and pepper; pour over artichokes. Chill, spooning marinade over a few times. Drain; dash with paprika. Arrange with lemon slices to serve.

ARTICHOKES MARINATED GREEK STYLE

2 packages frozen artichoke hearts
  Water
  Olive oil
  Lemon juice

Cook artichoke hearts according to package directions. Then let them cool. Pour over them a boiling hot marinade composed of remaining ingredients. Let the ar-

Salt
Peppercorns
Fennel
Thyme
Bay leaves
Celery seeds

tichokes cool off in this marinade and then place them in the refrigerator in their container. Serve them cold with their sauce.

MARINATED ARTICHOKES

1 package frozen artichoke hearts
1 tsp. chopped parsley
1/2 clove garlic, minced
Salad or olive oil
2 cups water
1 cup white vinegar
1 tsp. salt

Bring water, vinegar and salt to boil. Empty frozen artichoke hearts into cooker then remove from stove and allow to remain in cooker for 3 to 4 minutes. Remove, drain and cool thoroughly. Mix with chopped parsley, minced garlic to suit taste and add salad or olive oil.

PICKLED ARTICHOKES

About 6½ doz. artichokes, each about 2 by 3 inches
Acidified water
3 quarts water
3 cups white wine vinegar
4-1/2 tsp. salt
6 medium-sized or 12 small whole dried hot red chiles
6 medium-sized or 12 small garlic cloves
About ¾ cup minced parsley (optional)

Prepare artichokes according to Method 2. When all artichokes are trimmed, combine the 3 quarts of water, wine vinegar, and salt in a large pan and bring to a boil. Add drained artichokes, return to boil, then simmer until barely tender, about 10 minutes. With a slotted spoon, lift hot artichokes from water and arrange in hot sterilized wide mouth jars; a pint will hold 12 to 13 artichokes, a half-pint will hold 6 or 7. To each pint add 1 medium-sized red chile, 1 medium sized garlic clove, and 2 tbsp. parsley (if you wish). To each half-pint add a small chile, small garlic clove and 1 tbsp. parsley. Bring cooking water to a boil and pour into jars to cover artichokes; there should be about ¼ inch space to the rim of each jar. Seal. Store in a cool dark place for a month before using. Makes 6 pints or 12 half-pints.

PICKLED MUSHROOMS AND ARTICHOKES

2 (6 oz.) cans mushroom caps
1 package frozen artichoke hearts
3/4 cup olive oil
1/3 cup lemon juice
1/4 cup chopped parsley
1 clove garlic, crushed
1 tsp. salt
1/2 tsp. freshly ground black pepper

Drain cans of mushroom caps. Cook artichokes according to package directions. Drain and cool. Pack mushroom caps and artichoke hearts in 2 (12 oz.) sterilized jars. Cover with marinade made by combining olive oil, lemon juice, chopped parsley, garlic, salt and pepper. Seal tightly. Store at least 2 days before using. Serve on salads or with cocktails.

PICKLED

12 small artichokes
2 cups water
1/2 cup garlic-flavored vinegar
1 tsp. salt

Prepare artichokes according to Method 2. Combine water, vinegar and salt. Add artichokes, cover and cook 15 to 25 minutes until tender. Drain and marinate in French dressing before serving. Slice in half lengthwise and serve on salads or as appetizers.

QUICK MARINATED ARTICHOKES

6 medium sized artichokes (cooked)
1/2 cup olive oil or salad oil
5 cloves garlic, minced or mashed
1/2 cup chopped fresh parsley
1/4 cup lemon juice
1/2 tsp. salt
Dash of pepper
Chicory or other salad greens

Prepare artichokes according to Method 1. Spread apart the leaves of the cooked artichokes. Combine the oil with garlic, parsley. lemon juice, salt and pepper. Pour the oil mixture over the artichokes and continue to pour through the artichokes until the leaves are well coated. Return artichokes to the pan and simmer them for 10 minutes in the oil mixture. Let stand at room temperature at least 1 hour before serving. Arrange on individual plates garnished with sprigs of chicory.   Serves 6.

MARINATED HEARTS

4 pounds small artichokes
1 cup each olive oil and white vinegar

Prepare artichokes according to Method 2. You should have one quart of trimmed hearts. Add oil,

1   each whole carrot, small onion, celery stalk
2   cloves garlic
1   small stick cinnamon
5   bay leaves
1/2 tsp. each whole black peppers and salt

vinegar, carrot, onion, celery, garlic, cinnamon, bay leaves, whole peppers, and salt. Cover and bring to a boil, reduce heat, and simmer until tender, about 20 minutes. Let stand in cooking liquid, covered, overnight. Remove onion, bay leaves, and celery. Cut artichokes in half or leave very small ones whole, as you wish. Return to marinade and bring to a boil. With slotted spoon, lift artichokes from liquid; arrange in 2 wide-mouth pint jars or in a bowl. To each pint, add 1 or 2 slices of the carrot, half the cinnamon stick, and 1 clove garlic. Bring the remaining marinade to a boil. Cover the artichokes with the liquid. Store covered, in the refrigerator. Makes 2 pints.

ARTICHOKES IN LEMON BUTTER
1/2 cup minced onion
1/2 clove of garlic, crushed
2   tbsp butter
3/4 cup chicken broth
2   packages frozen artichoke hearts
3   tbsp. lemon juice
1/2 tsp. salt
1   tsp. oregano
1/4 tsp. grated lemon peel

Saute onion and garlic in butter until transparent; add broth and artichoke hearts. Season with lemon juice, salt, oregano and lemon peel. Simmer gently for 10 minutes or until artichokes are heated through.

Serves 6-8.

JEWISH STYLE
Small or medium-sized artichokes
Olive oil
Salt and pepper

Prepare artichokes according to Method 2. Heat olive oil (about 1 inch deep) in a deep, heavy frying pan at medium heat. Sprinkle centers of artichokes with salt and pepper. Place in hot oil; quickly brown on all sides. Turn artichokes upside down; press

tops firmly to bottom of frying pan to open leaves. Return to upright position. Reduce heat to low; continue cooking artichokes until tender when pierced with a fork (about 15 minutes). To give artichokes a fried crispness, wet hands with cold water and shake lightly over the artichokes while boiling it in oil, spraying it, leave artichokes in the pan for another minute. Drain on paper towels. Serve hot, one artichoke per person.

ARTICHOKE BARIGOULE

6 small or medium arti-
chokes
6 tbsp. olive oil
1 onion, chopped
2 cloves garlic, chopped
1 carrot, chopped
1 tbsp. minced parsley
1/2 tsp. rosemary
1 cup dry white table wine

Prepare artichokes according to Method 2. Cut in half lengthwise. place in saucepan with olive oil, onion, garlic, carrot, parsley and rosemary. Cover and cook, shaking pan a few times, until onion is golden. Add wine; cover and cook until artichokes are tender, about 30 minutes. Serve with sauce from pan.

Serves 6.

Artichokes always enhance the flavor of egg dishes, such as omelets and souffles, or scrambled eggs. The addition of sliced or chopped mushrooms and green peppers will further add to your enjoyment of this unusual combination. Egg dishes make for a perfect luncheon or supper entree as an accompaniment to cold meats.

ARTICHOKE SOUFFLE

1-1/2 cups artichoke pulp
1   onion, chopped finely
1   clove garlic, minced
1/2 bell pepper, finely chopped
1   tsp. Italian herbs
1   tsp. salt
1/2 tsp. pepper
1   tomato, peeled, seeded and chopped
1   cup well seasoned white sauce
1/2 cup grated Cheddar cheese
10 eggs, separated

Prepare artichokes according to Method 6. Saute onion, garlic, bell pepper, Italian herbs, salt, pepper and tomato. In a large mixing bowl add artichoke pulp, white sauce and Cheddar cheese. Add sauted ingredients. Add slightly beaten egg yolks and mix well. Beat egg whites until stiff and fold into mixture. Place mixture in a casserole dish and then set casserole in pan of water. Bake at 350° for 1 hour or until set.

Serves 6.

FRITTATA AL CARCIOFO

1   package artichoke hearts cooked and cut in half
3   tbsp. olive oil
1   clove garlic, minced
1   medium onion, thinly sliced
8   eggs
2   slices bread, soaked in water, squeezed dry
Salt and pepper
1/4 cup minced parsley

Cook garlic and onion in olive oil in large skillet over low heat until onion is soft and yellow. Beat eggs lightly and add crumbled bread, salt, and pepper, herbs, cheese and artichoke hearts. Pour into skillet and cook over low heat until sides come away from the pan (8-10 min.) Turn and cook second side 6-8 min., finish under

1/4 tsp. dried rosemary or 1 tsp. fresh
1/2 cup grated Parmesan cheese

low broiler flame.

Serves 4.

CURRIED ARTICHOKES AND EGGS

1/2 package frozen artichoke hearts
4 eggs, slightly beaten
3/4 cup milk
1 tsp. curry powder
1 tbsp. finely chopped onion
1 tsp. salt
1/4 cup melted butter or margarine

Cook artichokes according to package direction and chop. Combine eggs, milk, curry powder, onion and salt. Mix in blender. Stir in chopped artichoke. Melt butter; add egg mixture. Cook over low heat, stirring constantly, until set. Garnish with tomato wedges, if desired.

Serves 4.

EGGS SARDOU

1 cup creamed spinach, hot
2 artichoke bottoms, cooked
2 poached eggs
3/4 cup Hollandaise sauce

On a base of creamed spinach, place artichoke bottoms. Fill these with 2 poached eggs and cover with Hollandaise sauce.

Hollandaise Sauce:

4 egg yolks
Juice of 1 lemon
1/2 lb. melted butter
1/4 tsp salt

Beat egg yolks, add lemon juice. Heat in double boiler, add melted butter. Cook over very low fire until thick, stirring with wooden spoon. Salt to taste.

ARTICHOKE BOTTOMS WITH EGGS AND CREAM

4 large artichokes
4 tbsp. chopped fines herbs
1 cup heavy cream
Juice of 1/2 lemon
4 soft-cooked eggs
Salt and pepper

Prepare and cook artichokes according to Method 5. Place on a small serving platter. Combine half the chopped fines herbs (parsley, chervil, tarragon) with 2½ tbsp. of very heavy cream and the juice of ½ lemon. Spoon the moisture into the artichoke bottoms. Place an egg on each artichoke bottom. Whip the rest of the cream. Season with salt, pepper, and the rest of the herbs. Heap this on top of the eggs.

Chill in the refrigerator. This dish should be served very cold on lettuce cups.   Serves 4.

ARTICHAUTS SOUFFLE

2   tbps. butter
2   tbsp. flour
1   cup cream (or ¾ cup cream and ¼ cup milk)
4   beaten egg yolks
1   cup cooked artichoke bottoms
    Salt and pepper
4   egg whites

Melt butter, then remove from the heat. Rub in flour until completely free from lumps. When well blended, add cream. Stir constantly until thickened. Boil over lowest possible heat for two minutes, stirring constantly. Cool. When well cooled, add well-beaten egg yolks and cooked artichoke bottoms. Season with salt and pepper to taste. Beat egg whites until stiff. Fold into the mixture carefully. Pour into a 1-quart greased, glass baking dish. Place baking dish in a pan of hot water and bake in a 325° oven for approximately 30 minutes. Serves 4.

ARTICHOKES FLEMISH STYLE

1   package frozen artichoke hearts
4   egg yolks
1   cup heavy cream
2   tbsp. chopped parsley
2   tbsp. lemon juice
    Salt and pepper to taste

Thaw artichoke hearts and cut into quarters. Beat together egg yolks, cream and parsley in saucepan. Stir over low heat until sauce thickens slightly. Add artichokes and heat to serving temperature. Stir in lemon juice, salt and pepper. Serve at once garnished with additional parsley.   Serves 4.

ARTICHOKES WITH EGGS

2   tbsp. salad oil or butter
2   cups chopped marinated artichoke hearts
6 to 8 eggs
    Sliced tomatoes
1/2 tsp. salt

Heat oil or butter in a 10-12 inch frying pan. Add marinated artichoke hearts and stir until hot. Beat eggs with salt. Pour over artichokes; scramble gently until eggs are set. Garnish with tomato slices.   Serves 4.

ARTICHOKE OMELET II

1/2 package frozen artichoke hearts
1/4 cup olive oil

Cut artichoke hearts into ½-inch pieces lengthwise. Heat olive oil in a skillet, add artichokes, garlic

1   clove garlic, minced
2-4 tsp. parsley
1   onion, thinly sliced
4   eggs
    Salt and pepper

and parsley. Cook, stirring frequently until lightly browned. Add onion and cook a little longer. Beat the eggs slightly with the salt and pepper and pour over artichoke mixture. Cook very slowly until browned on bottom, turn out on large frying pan lid, then slide back into pan and brown on the other side. Cut into wedges. Serves 4.

SCRAMBLED EGGS WITH ARTICHOKE HEARTS

1   jar marinated artichoke
    hearts
1/4 lb. fresh mushrooms
3   tbsp. chopped parsley
6   eggs, beaten with 3 tbsp.
    milk
2   tbsp. melted butter or margarine

Drain artichoke hearts and pour oil in skillet. Slice mushrooms and artichokes. Saute together with parsley until thoroughly heated. Push to one side of skillet and add butter. Allow to melt and pour in well beaten eggs. Gently stir the whole mixture and cook slowly until eggs are set. Serve immediately on hot plates with catsup.   Serves 4.

SCRAMBLED HEARTS

3   small artichokes
2   tbsp. butter or margarine
2   tbsp. chopped onions
6   eggs
1/2 tsp. salt
1/2 cup milk

Prepare artichokes according to Method 2. Cut artichokes into lengthwise slices. Melt butter in frying pan and add artichokes. Cover and cook slowly until tender, about 15 minutes. Stir frequently to prevent browning. Add onion a few minutes before artichokes are tender. Beat eggs with salt and milk and pour over artichokes. Cook slowly until set, stirring from the bottom as mixture cooks.   Serves 4.

ARTICHOKE OMELET I

8   small artichokes
3   tbsp. butter or margarine
    Salt
1/4 tsp. tarragon (optional)
3   eggs

Prepare artichokes according to Method 2. Cut artichokes in half lengthwise. If you use frozen artichokes, let them thaw. Cover and simmer until tender. Saute

71

artichokes in butter, season with salt to taste. Add crushed tarragon, if desired. Add 2 tbsp. artichokes to a 3-egg omelet before you cook it, or fill the same size omelet with 2 tbsp, of the cooked artichokes. Fold and serve with remaining artichokes.   Serves 2.

PARMESAN CUSTARD

2   packages frozen artichoke hearts
1/2 cup drained, canned tomatoes
1   tsp. salt
1/4 tsp. pepper
1/4 tsp. garlic salt
1/4 tsp. chopped parsley
1/2 cup grated Parmesan cheese
3/4 cup water
1/4 cup olive oil
6   eggs

Arrange unthawed artichoke hearts in the bottom of a greased 2-quart casserole. Cut up tomatoes over the top of the artichoke hearts. Sprinkle with salt and pepper, garlic salt, chopped parsley, and Parmesan cheese. Pour in water and olive oil. Cover and bake in a moderate oven (350°) for 1 hour, or until the artichokes are tender. Beat eggs with a rotary beater until light and fluffy, pour over the cooked artichokes, and continue baking uncovered until the eggs are set, about 15 to 20 minutes longer.   Serves 8.

BASQUE STYLE

6   large artichokes
    Boiling salted water
2   tbsp. lemon juice
3   tbsp. olive oil or salad oil
1/4 cup chopped onion
1   clove garlic, minced or mashed
1   can (1 lb.) tomatoes
1/2 cup halved, pitted ripe olives
1/2 tsp. each salt, thyme and oregano
    Dash of pepper
    Scrambled eggs
    Grated Parmesan cheese

Cut off the top third of each artichoke and prepare according to Method 1; boil, cool and remove choke. Stand artichokes in a shallow baking dish. Saute onion and garlic in remaining oil until soft; stir in tomatoes, olives, and seasonings. Bring to a boil, reduce heat, and simmer, uncovered, for about 20 minutes. Spoon sauce around artichokes in baking dish. Cover and bake in a moderate oven (350°) for about 10 minutes or until artichokes are thoroughly heated. To serve, fill artichokes with eggs.

Scrambled Eggs:

6 eggs
3 tbsp. half-and-half
1/2 tsp. salt
Dash pepper
2 tsp. chopped parsley
2 tbsp. butter

Beat eggs with half-and-half, salt, pepper and parsley. Melt butter in a frying pan; scramble eggs in butter over low heat until cooked to taste.

Serves 6.

FRITTATA

1 clove garlic, minced or mashed
1 large onion, chopped
Olive oil
2 packages frozen artichoke hearts
3 stalks celery, sliced
3 sprigs parsley, minced
1 can (4 oz.) sliced mushrooms, drained
3/4 tsp. each basil and oregano
1/2 can (10½ oz.) tomato soup
Salt and pepper to taste
5 eggs
1/2 cup milk
2 tbsp. grated Parmesan cheese
Paprika

Heat electric frying pan to 300° and saute garlic and onion in oil until limp. Add the artichoke hearts, celery, parsley, mushrooms, basil, oregano, and tomato soup. Season to taste with salt and pepper. Cover and cook until tender, about 15 minutes. Beat eggs and stir in milk. Spread vegetables evenly on frying pan and pour over the egg mixture. Sprinkle with grated cheese and paprika; cover and cook at 250° until eggs are set, 5 to 10 minutes.

Serves 6.

TORTA DE ALCACHOFA

1 package frozen artichoke hearts
1/4 cup oil
1 clove garlic
1 small onion, minced
1 sprig fresh sweet basil
4 eggs
3 tablespoons grated cheese
Salt and pepper to taste

Slice artichokes in half lengthwise. Put oil in pan, add peeled whole clove of garlic, minced onion and sliced artichokes. Cover and let cook until artichokes are tender. Beat eggs well, add cheese, pour over artichokes and with a fork keep stirring as you would scrambled eggs. Cook until egg is well cooked.

Serves 4 to 6.

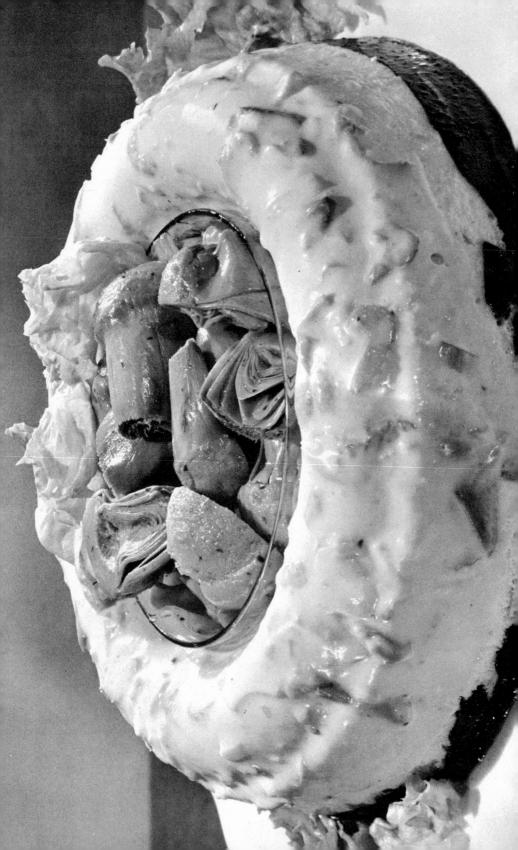

Artichokes when served in salads for a luncheon or dinner are the "piece de resistance" for any occasion.

PALACE COURT SALAD

1/2 cup finely shredded Iceburg lettuce
2 egg yolks of hardboiled eggs
slice of peeled tomato
1 cooked artichoke bottom
Crab salad
4 crab legs
2 half-inch strips of pimiento
1000 Island dressing

Arrange lettuce in a firm, round mound on a chilled serving plate. Sieve or rice the egg yolks and using a folded napkin, press firmly into the lettuce mound all around, leaving top free of egg. Set a thick tomato slice on lettuce base and top with an artichoke bottom. Fill bottom with a small amount of crab salad. Top with crab legs. Garnish with pimiento. Serve with dressing.

Serves 1.

ENSALADA DE ALCACHOFAS

1 package frozen artichoke hearts
1 tbsp. plain gelatin
1/2 cup French dressing
2/3 cup mayonnaise
5 hard-boiled eggs, chopped
1 cup cold water
1 tsp. salt
1/2 cup chili sauce
1/4 tsp. paprika
1/2 cup whipped cream
Sliced olives

Prepare artichoke hearts according to package directions. Chop hearts. Soften gelatin in cold water for a few minutes, then dissolve over hot water. Add to this the French dressing, chili sauce, salt, paprika, whipped cream and mayonnaise. Finally add eggs, olives and artichokes. Pour into mold and chill until firm. Remove from mold and serve on lettuce leaves.

RISOTTO SALAD

1 package (6-7 oz). chicken flavored rice mix

Cook rice as directed on the package, except omit the addition of

2 green onions, thinly sliced
1/2 green pepper, seeded and chopped
8 pimiento-stuffed green olives, sliced
2 jars marinated artichoke hearts
1/4 tsp. curry powder
1/3 cup mayonnaise
Romaine or butter lettuce
Radishes or tomato wedges for garnish (optional)

butter. Remove from heat, turn into a bowl, and let stand until cooled to room temperature. Add onions, green pepper, and olives to the rice. Drain artichoke hearts, reserving the marinade. Combine artichoke marinade with curry powder and mayonnaise; mix until blended. Add this dressing to the rice mixture along with the artichoke hearts; mix lightly. Cover bowl and refrigerate until well chilled. To serve, turn into a salad bowl or serving plate and garnish with romaine or butter lettuce. Arrange radishes or tomato wedges around the edge, if you wish. Serves 6-8.

STUFFED TOMATOES

8 ripe red tomatoes
Salt
1 jar marinated artichoke hearts
Lettuce
1 cup mayonnaise
1 tsp. anchovy paste
1 tsp. garlic vinegar
Anchovy fillets

Peel tomatoes, cut a slice from the top and scoop out the pulp. Sprinkle with salt, and drain upside down. Stuff each tomato with an artichoke heart. Arrange them on lettuce leaves, and pour over a dressing made by combining mayonnaise with anchovy paste and garlic vinegar. Garnish with crossed anchovy fiilets. Serves 8.

CRAB REMOULADE

4 artichoke bottoms, cooked
1 cup crab meat
Remoulade Sauce
Tomato slices
Lettuce cups
Capers

Chill artichoke bottoms. Place medium-thick tomato slices in lettuce cups; top each with a cooked chilled artichoke bottom, then about ¼ cup flaked crab meat. Top with Remoulade sauce; garnish with capers if desired.
Serves 4.

SHRIMP STUFFED I

6 medium artichokes, cooked
1/2 lb. small cooked shrimp
1/3 cup mayonnaise
1/4 cup sour cream

Prepare whole artichokes for stuffing according to Method 1. Cover and chill. For dressing, mix together mayonnaise, sour cream,

76

1-1/2 tbsp. lemon juice
1/2 tsp. grated lemon peel
1/4 tsp. salt
1/4 tsp. tarragon
1/4 tsp. Dijon-style mustard

lemon juice, grated lemon peel, salt, tarragon, and mustard. Just before serving, spoon 2 tbsp. dressing into the center of each artichoke and distribute shrimp on top of the dressing. Garnish with lemon wedges.

Serves 6.

CRAB STUFFED

4   large artichokes
     Salt
     French dressing
1-1/2 cups prepared crab meat
     Pepper
1-1/2 cups sliced celery
1/3 cup stuffed green olives
1/3 cup mayonnaise
1   tbsp. lemon juice

Prepare whole artichokes for stuffing according to Method 1. Gently spread outer leaves apart to form broad shallow cup. Drizzle French dressing over artichokes and chill. Combine crab, celery and sliced olives. Blend mayonnaise and lemon juice and pour over crab mixture. Toss together lightly with salt and pepper. Heap into chilled artichokes.

Serves 4.

IN ASPIC

1-3/4 cups tomato juice
1   envelope (1 tbsp.) plain gelatin
1   tbsp. vinegar
1   tsp. grated onion
1/2 tsp. salt
1   hard-boiled egg
3   cooked artichoke hearts
1/2 cup chopped celery
     Salad greens
     Mayonnaise
     Dash of Worcestershire sauce

Prepare artichokes according to Method 2. Heat 1½ cups tomato juice. Soften gelatin in remaining cold tomato juice and dissolve in hot juice. Blend in vinegar, onion, salt and Worcestershire sauce. Cool to consistency of unbeaten egg white. Slice egg and artichoke hearts crosswise. In 6 individual molds, place a slice of egg and a slice of artichoke. Cover with thin layer of gelatin mixture and chill. Chop remaining egg and artichoke and fold into rest of gelatin with celery. Turn into molds over firm layer and chill until firm. Unmold on salad greens and serve with mayonnaise.

Serves 6.

HEART SALAD

1 cup Italian Dressing (page 109)
1 package frozen artichoke hearts
1 4-oz. can or jar pimientos, chopped
1 2-oz. can anchovy fillets, diced
2 cups torn head lettuce
2 cups torn romaine
2 cups torn spinach

Heat dressing to boiling; add artichokes; cook till tender, about 3 to 5 minutes. Cool. Stir in pimiento and anchovies. Chill in dressing till serving time. Drain off dressing and reserve. Add artichoke mixture to greens, toss with enough reserved dressing to coat greens.

Serves 8.

CRAB SALAD

16 crab legs or 1 cup flaked crab meat
1 cup sour cream
2 tbsp. minced chives
1 cup marinated artichoke hearts or 6 oz. jar
Juice of 1 lemon
Lettuce
Salt

Place a thick wedge of crisp head lettuce on each of 8 individual salad plates. Blend together sour cream, chives, and lemon juice. Cut artichoke hearts in small pieces and add to sour cream mixture with marinade oil. Season with salt. Spoon an equal amount on each serving of lettuce. Garnish each with 1 or 2 crab legs (or instead, blend crab meat with dressing).

Serves 8.

ARTICHAUTS A LA BARIGOULE

4 artichokes, medium-size
2 cups leftover cooked turkey, chicken, shrimp, lobster or crab meat
1 cup chopped celery
1/4 cup minced green pepper
2 tbsp. grated onion
1 tbsp. chopped parsley
2 tbsp. olive oil
1 tbsp. vinegar or lemon juice
Mayonnaise

Prepare whole artichokes for stuffing according to Method 1. Combine poultry or fish, chopped celery, green pepper, onion, parsley, olive oil, and vinegar or lemon juice. Spread leaves of artichokes outward and stuff by filling center with salad mixture. Decorate each with a generous tbsp. of mayonnaise. To eat, remove leaves one by one and dip them in mayonnaise, leaving remaining salad to be eaten with artichoke heart. Serve on bed of salad greens.

Serves 4.

GREEN EGGS MAYONNAISE ON ARTICHOKE BOTTOMS

12 eggs, poached until whites are firm
1/2 bunch watercress
12 sprigs parsley
2/3 lb. spinach leaves
1 tsp. each dried tarragon and chervil
Boiling water
2 cups mayonnaise
1 envelope (1 tbsp.) unflavored gelatin
2 cups chicken consomme
12 cooked fresh or frozen artichoke bottoms, chilled

Remove poached eggs from pan; drain and cool. Immerse watercress, parsley, spinach, tarragon, and chervil in boiling water for a few minutes (to bring out the bright green color). Drain well, press out water between paper towels. Place in blender with mayonnaise just long enough to pulverize the greens. Trim ragged edges from eggs; set them on a rack over a shallow pan. Coat top of each with green mayonnaise and garnish with a pickled mushroom. Chill. Soften gelatin in consomme; heat until gelatin dissolves. Cool until syrupy; spoon a little of the gelatin over each egg to coat thinly. Chill eggs. Pour remainder of gelatin mixture into a pan in a layer ½-inch thick; chill. When set, cut into ½-inch thick cubes. Set each egg in an artichoke bottom; garnish with cubed gelatin mixture. Serve them (one to a person) as a dinner first course or on buffet table, or (two to a person) for a luncheon or supper main dish.

Serves 6.

PIMIENTO CUPS

1 small jar marinated artichokes
1 can (4 oz.) whole pimientos
1 cup finely minced celery
3 chopped anchovies
2 tbsp. minced onions
1/3 cup mayonnaise
1/2 tsp. garlic salt
1/2 tsp. pepper

Drain pimientoes. Combine celery, anchovies, onion, and mayonnaise together. Season with salt and pepper. Fill the pimiento cups with the mixture and top with marinated artichokes. Arrange on individual plates, garnished with crisp greens.

Serves 4.

ARTICHOKE-GRAPEFRUIT SALAD

1   head crisp green lettuce
1   bunch endive
1   jar artichoke hearts
2   onions, sliced and separated into rings
2   grapefruit, sectioned
    Garlic French dressing or
    Roquefort dressing

Make a nest of lettuce and endive. Place artichoke hearts, onion rings and grapefruit sections on nest. Season with dressing.

Serves 6.

CARCIOFO SANTA CRUZ

6   artichokes
    Salt
1/4 lb. fresh mushrooms, chopped
1/2 cup chopped cucumbers
1/4 cup chopped green onions
2   tbsp. salad oil
1   6-oz. package frozen King crab meat, thawed and chopped
1/2 lb. cooked, cleaned shrimp, chopped
2   hard-boiled eggs, chopped
1/2 cup mayonnaise
1/2 cup sour cream
2   tbsp. chopped fresh dill or 1 tsp. dill weed
1/8 tsp. white pepper
2   tbsp. lemon juice

Prepare artichokes according to Method 4. Saute mushrooms and onions in oil until tender, but not browned. In large bowl, combine mushrooms with cucumbers, crab meat, shrimp, eggs, mayonnaise, sour cream, dill, 1 tsp. salt, pepper and lemon juice. Chill; fill prepared artichokes with salad. Serve garnished on lettuce cups with lemon wedges and parsley as desired.

Serves 6.

SHRIMP STUFFED II

8   large artichokes
    Tart French dressing
1/3 cup mayonnaise
1   tbsp. lemon juice
1-1/2 cups cooked, cleaned shrimp
1/3 cup pitted ripe olives, sliced
1-1/2 cups diced celery
    Salt
    Pepper
    Paprika

Prepare whole artichokes for stuffing according to Method 1. Cool. Gently spread the outer leaves to form a cup, and scoop out the choke. Cover each artichoke with French dressing, and chill. When ready to serve, Combine mayonnaise and lemon juice, and toss lightly with shrimp, olives, and celery. Heap into artichoke cups, and sprinkle with salt, pepper and paprika. Serve chilled.   Serves 8.

ARTICHOKE AND CRAB COCKTAIL

1 cup diced, cooked
   artichoke hearts
1 cup crab meat
1/2 cup cream
1 cup mayonnaise
1/2 cup catsup
1/2 tsp. Worcestershire

Mix artichoke hearts and crab meat; chill. Whip cream and combine with mayonnaise, catsup, Worcestershire sauce. Season, chill and combine with first mixture.

Serves 6.

MIXED TUNA SALAD STUFFING

2 cans tuna
1 cup chopped celery
1/2 cup chopped green onion
   Mayonnaise
4 artichokes
4 tomatoes
4 hard-boiled eggs
   Lemon wedges

Prepare artichokes according to Method 4. Drain oil from tuna. Flake the fish and combine it with the celery and onion. Blend with mayonnaise to taste and fill artichoke casings. Wash tomatoes and cut them in quarters. Quarter the eggs and arrange these around the artichokes. Serve with additional mayonnaise and lemon wedges.

Serves 4.

ARTICHOKE DECORATO

12 large artichokes
1 cup bread-and-butter
   pickles
2 hard-boiled eggs
2 medium tomatoes
1 cup French dressing
1/2 tsp. oregano
1/2 tsp. thyme

Prepare artichokes according to Method 4. Then arrange on a flat platter, cover with wax paper and place in the refrigerator. When ready to serve, fill the centers with the solids in the sauce and pour the liquid dressing over them.

Sauce: Chop pickles, eggs and tomatoes. Combine.

Dressing: Add French dressing, oregano and thyme. Stir gently until combined.

Wonderful addition for a buffet.

Serves 12.

WESTERN SALAD BOWL

1/2 package frozen artichoke
   hearts, thawed
1 small head lettuce
1 bunch Romaine
2 green onions

Break salad greens in bite-sized pieces into salad bowl. Add halved or quartered artichoke hearts and thinly sliced green onions. Sprinkle with oil and vinegar and toss

81

1/4 cup salad oil
2 tomatoes
2 tbsp. garlic flavored wine vinegar
1 hard-boiled egg
Pepper

lightly until greens are thoroughly coated. Add tomato wedges and slices of eggs.

Serves 8.

RED AND WHITE SALAD

1 jar marinated artichoke hearts
1 envelope gelatin
1/4 cup cold liquid (oil from artichoke hearts and water)
1 tbsp. vinegar
1/2 cup boiling water
1/2 pint whipping cream
1 cup salad dressing (mayonnaise type)
2 eggs; hard boiled and chopped
1 cup celery, chopped
1 can chicken, tuna, turkey, shrimp or crab
1 package raspberry jello (not black raspberry)
2 cups tomato juice

Drain artichokes, reserving liquid. Add additional cold water to bring liquid measurement to ¼ cup. Add to gelatin and allow to soak. Add vinegar and boiling water; stir to dissolve. Whip cream, fold into mayonnaise and mix into gelatin. Add eggs, celery, meat and artichoke hearts. Pour into a 6 x 9 inch loaf pan, ring mold or 9 inch square pan. While this mixture is setting, make a second layer. Dissolve raspberry jello in 1 cup heated tomato juice. Stir in 1 cup cold tomato juice. When cool and as firm as loose jelly, pour over white layer. Chill. Cut salad into squares and serve on lettuce cup. Garnish with slices of stuffed green olives. Serves 8.

ITALIAN VEGETABLE SALAD

2 jars marinated artichoke hearts, drain (save oil)
1 can kidney beans, drained
1 can garbanzo beans, drained
3 stalks celery, cut diagonally
4 par-cooked carrots, sliced thin
String beans, peas, and any other par-cooked vegetable that you might choose

Combine the ingredients for marinating oil and allow to stand for 3 to 4 hours before serving. Add vegetable-bean combination and allow to stand at least one hour before serving.

When serving, top with any additional vegetables you might care to use; such as tomatoes, avacado, additional artichoke hearts, shrimp, salami and wedges of cheese.   Serves 4.

Marinade Oil:
1   spray parsley, slightly crushed
2   cloves garlic, whole
1/4 cup Bermuda or any sweet onion, chopped fine
1   tsp. prepared mustard
3/4 or 1 tsp accent
    Salt and pepper
    Oil for artichoke hearts combined with half as much vinegar

JAIBA Y ALCACHOFA

1   cup diced, cooked artichoke hearts
1   cup crab meat
1/2 cup heavy cream, whipped
1   cup mayonnaise
1/2 cup tomato catsup
    dash of Tabasco sauce
    salt and pepper

Mix artichokes and crab meat; chill. Combine whipped cream, sauce, salt and pepper; chill. When ready to serve, combine sauce with the artichoke and crab mixture. Serve on lettuce. If desired, use cooked shrimp or lobster meat instead of crab, and add ¼ cup chopped ripe or green olives.

Serves 6.

ALCACHOFAS A LA VINAGRETA
1   package artichoke hearts
2   onions cut into rings (preferably red onions)
3/4 cup oil
1/2 cup vinegar
1   teaspoon prepared mustard
    salt and pepper

Cook artichoke according to package directions. Drain. In a deep bowl arrange alternate layers of artichokes and onion rings. Mix remaining ingredients, pour over the artichokes and onions and let stand several hours before serving. Turn artichokes occasionally so that they will be well coated with the dressing.

Serves 3 or 4.

Soups

If you have never tasted artichoke soup before, you are missing a rare treat. Served either hot or cold it has a delightfully unusual flavor that is the perfect gourmet touch to any meal.

CONSOMME AUX ARTICHAUTS

1   cup artichoke pulp
1-1/2 cups Bechamel sauce
1-1/2 cups boullion
      Salt and pepper

Prepare artichokes according to Method 6. Make the Bechamel sauce. Mix with the boullion. Combine the artichoke pulp with the boullion mixture and season with salt and pepper. Chill in the refrigerator. Serve the soup in individual soup bowls and garnish with parsley.   Serves 4.

CREAM OF ARTICHOKE SOUP

1-1/2 cups artichoke pulp
6-1/2 cups thin Bechamel
      sauce
1   cup scalded milk
1/2 cup heavy cream
      Salt and pepper
      Croutons, fried in butter
      (optional)

Prepare artichokes according to Method 6. Make the thin Bechamel sauce. Add artichoke pulp and hot milk and stir well. Season to taste and reheat, adding the cream. Serve hot and, if you like, serve a little bowl of croutons, fried in butter.   Serves 6.

ARTICHOKE SOUP

2   cups artichoke pulp
2   cups chicken stock
      Milk or cream
      Salt and pepper

Prepare artichokes according to Method 6. Cook pulp and chicken stock together; add milk or cream until thinned to the desired consistency and season with salt and pepper to taste. This is good either chilled or hot.   Serves 4.

Appetizers

Artichokes are delightful as appetizers. Each leaf can be an edible container for a tasty morsel of cheese or shrimp and arranged on your tray to resemble a sunflower. Marinated artichoke hearts skewered with toothpicks and dunked in appropriate sauces or any of the following suggestions will surely bring praise to the hostess.

SKEWERED HEARTS AND MUSHROOMS

1 package frozen artichoke hearts (halved)
2 dozen small mushrooms
Consomme
Gruyere cheese (grated)
Parmesan cheese (grated)
1 hard-boiled egg
1 cup melted butter
Salt and pepper
Anchovy paste
1 tsp. minced parsley
1 tsp. minced chives

Cook artichokes until tender in a well seasoned consomme. Drain. Dip the artichokes and mushrooms in melted butter, then roll them in equal parts of grated Gruyere and Parmesan cheese, seasoned with salt and pepper. Glaze the artichokes and mushrooms quickly under the oven broiler on a fireproof platter. Serve at once, pouring over them the following sauce: Saute a finely chopped hard-boiled egg in a little butter, and when mixture foams, stir in small amount of anchovy paste, which has been kneaded with minced parsley and minced chives. Skewer with toothpicks and serve hot.

PAN OR DEEP FRIED ARTICHOKE HEARTS

1 package frozen artichoke hearts, thawed
2 well beaten eggs
Flour
Garlic salt

Dip artichokes into beaten eggs, then roll in flour seasoned with garlic salt and pepper. Fry slowly in ¼ inch deep hot oil until golden brown on both sides. Serve

Pepper
Cooking oil

hot with lemon wedges or mayonnaise.

TEMPURA

1 package frozen artichoke hearts
1 egg
Salt and pepper
3 tbsp. flour
Oil for deep frying

Prepare artichokes according to Method 2. Beat eggs, add artichokes and toss until coated. Sprinkle with salt, pepper and flour mix until well coated. Fry in deep hot oil (360°) 10 to 15 minutes. Drain on absorbent paper and serve hot.   Serves 6.

SHRIMP AND CREAM CHEESE

1 large artichoke
Water
1 tsp. olive oil
1 bay leaf, crushed
1/2 tsp. salt
1 package (3 oz.) cream cheese
1/4 tsp. garlic powder
About 2 tbsp. cream
About 1/4 pound small shrimp
Paprika
1/4 tsp. liquid hot pepper seasoning

Cook the artichoke according to Method 1, then remove the leaves. Use the leaves that are firm enough to handle and have a good edible portion on the ends. Blend the cream cheese with hot-pepper seasoning, garlic powder, salt to taste, and cream to make a smooth paste. Spread this filling on the tip of each leaf. Place a small shrimp on top of the filling and sprinkle with paprika. Arrange on a round plate or tray in the shape of a sunflower so each leaf is easy to pick up.
Makes about 18.

RED CAVIAR

8 large artichokes or artichoke bottoms, cooked
8 tbsp. sour cream
1 can red caviar
Lettuce, sliced

Prepare artichokes according to Method 5. Allow I artichoke bottom for each person. Arrange on small plate, garnish with sliced (not chopped) lettuce, and fill each artichoke bottom with 1 generous tbsp. sour cream, and top with 1 tsp. red caviar.
Serves 8.

ARTICHOKE HEARTS CRISP FRIED

1   package frozen artichoke hearts, thawed
1   egg
1/2 cup milk
1/2 cup flour
1/2 tsp. baking powder
    Salt and pepper to taste
    Cooking oil

Quarter artichoke hearts. Make batter with egg, milk, flour, baking powder, salt and pepper. Dip hearts in batter and fry in hot oil until golden brown. Serve hot.

ARTICHOKE HEARTS GREEK STYLE

1   package frozen artichoke hearts
1   medium carrot, peeled and cubed
1   small potato, peeled and cubed
1   tbsp lemon juice
1   cup water
1/4 cup olive oil
1/2 tsp. salt
1   tbsp. flour

Place vegetables and water in saucepan; add oil, salt and ½ tbsp. lemon juice. Cover and cook for 7 to 10 minutes or until tender. Remove vegetables. Thicken stock with flour. Cook until smooth and thickened. Add remaining lemon juice. Pour sauce over vegetables. Chill. Serve cold.
Serves 6 to 8.

FONDS D'ARTICHAUTS

1   package frozen artichoke hearts
1/2 tsp. salt
2   tsp. olive oil
1/2 clove garlic
    Parsley
2   tbsp. vinegar
    Pepper
1   cup water

Place artichoke hearts in a saucepan. Add all ingredients. Cover and bring quickly to a boil over high heat. Then reduce heat and boil gently until just about tender, 7 to 12 minutes. Serve hot or cold.

HOT HORS D'OEUVRES

1   jar marinated artichoke hearts
6   slices bacon, cut in half

Partially broil 12 pieces of bacon. Drain on paper. Wrap each piece around an artichoke heart, fastening with a toothpick. Place under the broiler until bacon is crispy and artichokes are hot. Serve immediately.

ARTICHOKE FRITTERS

3 eggs, well beaten
1/2 tsp salt
1/2 tsp. pepper
1 cup canned milk
1 small onion, chopped fine
1/2 clove garlic, minced
1/2 cup grated Parmesan
cheese
1/2 cup flour
1 tsp. baking powder
6 white crackers ground fine
2 packages frozen artichoke
hearts, coarsely chopped

Combine all ingredients and let stand for approximately 10 minutes. Drop by teaspoons into hot deep fat and cook until brown and crisp.

COEURS D'ARTICHAUTS POMPADOUR

1 jar artichoke bottoms
Foies gras
Bread crumbs
Gruyere cheese, grated
Flaky pie crust

Drain artichoke bottoms; trim so that the artichoke will stand level. Fill the bottoms with a little foies gras previously rubbed through a fine sieve, sprinkle tops with equal parts o f seived bread crumbs and finely grated Gruyere cheese, and brown quickly under the broiler of the oven. Serve as hot as possible on small rounds of baked flaky pie crust.

ARTICHOKE COCKTAIL

Artichoke bottoms, cooked
French dressing, made
with lime juice instead of
vinegar
Lime

Cut artichoke bottoms in small cubes and marinate in French dressing. Serve in chilled cocktail glasses with a piece of lime on the side.

OLIVES AND SOUR CREAM

2 small packages (3 oz.)
softened cream cheese
Few drops garlic juice
1/4 cup commercial sour
cream
2 tsp. wine vinegar
1/4 cup minced ripe olives

Prepare artichokes according to Method 1—DO NOT trim tops. Wreath a plate with several layers of cooked artichoke leaves, tips pointing out. Combine sauce ingredients. Mix well, adding a few drops cream if necessary to

Salt to taste
4   medium-sized artichokes

make sauce the proper consistency for dunking. In the center of the artichoke leaves, put a bowlful of the sauce.

Serves 6.

ARTICHOKE TURNOVERS

Rich biscuit dough or pastry made with 2 cups flour
1   cup mashed artichoke pulp (3 to 4 large artichokes)
1/4 cup (4 tbsp.) canned cream of chicken soup, undiluted
2   slices crisp bacon, crumbled
Dash of pepper
1/2 tsp. Worcestershire sauce
1/2 tsp. prepared mustard
2/3 cup (about ¼ lb.)grated Cheddar cheese

Roll out biscuit dough ¼-inch thick (or pastry ⅛-inch thick), and cut into eight 4-inch circles. Mix together artichoke pulp, soup, bacon, pepper, Worcestershire, and mustard. Put 2 tbsp. of artichoke mixture on each circle of dough and top with heaping tbsp. of cheese. Fold dough over as for turnovers, and press edges together to seal. Bake in a very hot oven (450°) for 12 minutes. Makes 8 turnovers. These make tasty tidbits for hot hors d'oeuvres. Prepare as above, but cut pastry into 2-inch or 3-inch circles.

FRITO MISTO

1/2 package frozen artichoke hearts
3   eggs
1-1/2 tsp. garlic salt
1-1/2 tsp. monosodium glutamate
1/4 tsp. Tabasco
3   tbsp. salad oil
1   cup milk
1-1/2 cups flour
8   tomato wedges, floured
8   cauliflower buds, cooked crisp tender, and drained
1/2 lb whole green beans, cooked crisp tender, and drained
1   lb. chicken livers, floured
Salad oil for frying

Combine and beat eggs, seasonings, and oil; add milk. Mix in flour. Quarter artichoke hearts. Dip vegetables and livers in batter. Deep fry in heated oil at 360°, 3 to 8 minutes, turning to brown on all sides. Drain on paper towels.

Serves 4-6.

ALCACHOFAS EMPANIZADAS

1   package frozen artichoke
    hearts
3   eggs
    fine bread crumbs
    grated cheese
    salt and pepper

Cook artichokes until tender according to package directions. Drain. When cold cut in halves lengthwise, dip in beaten eggs, then into bread crumbs which have been mixed with grated cheese. Salt and pepper to taste. Repeat this egging-and-crumbing, and fry in generous amounts of oil in a skillet until brown on both sides.

Serves 8.

Specialties

The following recipes will be of interest to the gourmet chef who has been searching for something truly unusual.

ARTICHOKE SPICE CAKE OR CUP CAKES

2   cups artichoke pulp
2   cups flour
1   tsp. baking powder
1 tsp. baking soda
1/2 tsp. nutmeg
1/2 tsp. cinnamon
1/2 tsp. cloves
1/2 tsp. salt
1-1/2 cups sugar
1/2 cup salad oil
2   egg yolks
1   cup chopped nuts
1   cup raisins
2   egg whites

Prepare artichokes according to Method 6. Sift together the flour, baking powder, baking soda, nutmeg, cinnamon, cloves and salt. Combine artichoke pulp, sugar, oil, egg yolks, nuts and raisins. Pour into dry ingredients, beat until smooth. Beat egg white until stiff, fold into cake mixture. Pour into greased 13 x 9 inch pan, bake at 350° for 40 to 45 minutes until tested done. Or, pour batter into prepared cup cake tins, bake at 350° for 20 25 minutes.

ARTICHOKE RING

1-1/2 cups artichoke pulp
4   eggs, separated
1/2 cup cracker crumbs
1   tsp. lemon juice
1   tsp. scraped onion
    Salt and pepper
1   cup cream

Prepare artichokes according to Method 6. To the artichoke pulp add the egg yolks, beaten, cracker crumbs, lemon juice, scraped onion, and salt and pepper to taste. Beat egg whites until stiff, but not dry, and fold into the artichoke mixture, along with cream, whipped and a few grains of salt. Pour into a well-greased 1½-quart mold, and bake in a pan of water in a moderate oven (350°) for 45 minutes, or until a knife, inserted, comes out clean. Cool very slightly and turn out on a hot round platter. Fill artichoke ring with creamed fish, shellfish, or poultry. You will find it particularly good with crab meat, sprinkled with toasted almonds; or with chicken in a white wine sauce.

ARTICHOKE CAKE

2-1/2 cups regular flour
1 tsp. baking soda
1 tsp. salt
1 tsp. cinnamon
1/2 tsp. cloves
1 cup sugar
1/2 cup oil
2 eggs
1-1/2 cups artichoke pulp
1/2 cup raisins
1/2 cup nuts

Prepare artichokes according to Method 6. Measure dry ingredients and sift them into a bowl. Add shortening and artichoke pulp and beat for two minutes with an electric beater or 150 strokes by hand. Add unbeaten eggs and beat for two minutes more. Fold in chopped nuts and raisins. Line a 9-inch square pan or two 8-inch layer cake pans with wax paper and bake in a moderate oven (350°) 30 to 35 minutes for square pan and 20 to 25 minutes for layers.

ARTICHOKE PIE

2 packages frozen artichoke hearts
1/4 cup minced onions
2 tsp. minced parsley
3 tbsp butter
2 tbsp. melted butter
2 tbsp. flour
1 cup half-and-half
1 tbsp. tarragon vinegar

Prepare a 2-crust pastry. Cook artichoke hearts according to package directions. Line an 8-inch pie pan with half of the pastry. Trim pastry and seal edge of rim of the pan. Add the drained artichoke hearts; sprinkle with minced onion and minced parsley. Dot with butter, top with crust (rolled thicker than usual so it will not break), and cut to fit top of pie. Lightly press top crust to trim of bottom crust but do not seal edges. Bake in a hot oven (425°) for 10 minutes; reduce heat to moderate (350°) and continue cooking 20 to 25 minutes longer, or until crust is brown. Just before time to serve pie, blend melted butter, flour, 1 cup half-and-half half milk and half cream), and cook until thick, stirring constantly. Then stir in, drop by drop, 1 tbsp. tarragon vinegar. Lift upper crust carefully and pour sauce over the filling. Replace top and serve at once. Serve for a luncheon or a light supper. Serves 6.

ARTICHOKE FRUIT CAKE

2 cups sugar
1/2 cup shortening
3 eggs
1 tsp. salt
1 tsp. allspice
1/2 cup milk
2 tsp. baking powder
2 tsp. vanilla
2 cups regular flour
1 cup raisins
1/2 cup nuts
1/2 cup mixed fruit (fruit cake mix)
1 tsp. lemon juice
2 cups artichoke pulp

Prepare artichokes according to Method 6. Measure dry ingredients and sift them into bowl. Add shortening, milk, artichoke pulp, lemon juice and beat for two minutes with an electric beater or 150 strokes by hand. Add unbeaten eggs and beat for two minutes more. Fold in chopped nuts, raisins and mixed fruit. Line a 10-inch square pan with wax paper and bake in a moderate oven (350°) for 30 to 35 minutes.

CREPES

1-1/2 cups flour
3 eggs
1-1/2 cups milk
1/4 cup water
2 tbsp. marinade oil
1/2 tbsp. salt

Mix all the ingredients and let stand for ½ hour. Then fry crepes in a slightly greased skillet (same size and procedure as used in making pancakes).

1 jar marinated artichoke hearts
1-1/2 cups cottage cheese, cream style
1 egg, well beaten
2 tbsp. sugar

Mix these engredients well and set aside while frying crepes.

1 cube butter

Melt butter and add cream. Bring

96

1-1/2 cups thin cream

IVAR

1   jar marinated artichoke hearts
4   green bell peppers
4   red bell peppers
1/2 cup cold water
1   clove of garlic
    Wine vinegar to taste
    Salt and pepper to taste

to a slow simmer in a casserole or Dutch oven. Fill each Crepe with 2 or 3 tbsp. of filling, roll up and lay them side by side in casserole. Cover casserole and bake at 375° for 35 minutes. Remove cover and continue cooking for 10 more minutes. Serve with sour cream or plain as preferred.

Serves 6.

Place peppers in a shallow pan and bake in a 400° oven for one hour until peppers are soft and skin starts to shrivel. Remove peppers from oven, place in a deep bowl and pour cold water over them. Cover with a dish towel for 20 minutes. Remove as much skin from peppers as possible. Chop peppers and garlic. Add artichoke hearts, that have been cut into small pieces, salt, pepper and wine vinegar to taste. Mix well and return to refrigerator until cold and ready to serve. Serve as relish with lamb or veal.

CARDOON

The cardoon is a thistle-like plant resembling the artichoke, but generally taller. Some varieties attain a height of eight to ten feet, with pale green leaves, often 3 feet long, covered with a silvery down. It is grown for the fleshy leaf midribs of the young plant which are cut into short lengths and cooked in boiling salted water until just tender. Keep the vegetable well covered with water to avoid its tendency to blacken. After draining, free from strings, (if any remain), and serve with a butter sauce, or a rich cream sauce, seasoning to taste with salt, pepper and a dash of nutmeg. The Italians prefer to bread the cooked pieces and saute them in olive oil; the oil is then drained off and a thick tomato sauce flavored with dill, fennel and plenty of garlic added. Cardoons may be dipped in a batter, then fried in deep fat. Also they may be used in salads, stews, soups, and casserole combinations.

CHEESE

Cardoons may also be prepared according to all the different methods applied to celery, but in all cases they must be blanched before the final cooking, in order to remove the skins and slime.

The sharp, piquant flavor of cheese in combination with artichokes will add a delightful Continental zest to your menu.

ARTICHOKE BOTTOMS A LA GRIMOD DE LA REYNIERE

4   large artichoke bottoms,
     cooked
4 to 5 onions (1 pound)
1/2 cup grated Gruyere cheese
3   tbsp. butter
     Tarragon
     Dry bread crumbs
     Salt and pepper

Prepare artichokes according to Method 5. Peel and slice the onions very fine and saute them in butter until golden. Season with tarragon, rosemary, salt and pepper; let cool. Fill the artichoke bottoms with the cold onions. Sprinkle with grated cheese and bread crumbs. Brown in the oven.   Serves 4.

AU GRATIN

8   cooked artichoke bottoms
1   cup milk
2   tbsp. flour
     Salt
     White pepper
     Nutmeg
1   cup grated Swiss cheese
     Milk
     Parmesan cheese
2   tbsp. butter

Fill a flameproof casserole with artichoke bottoms. Make a white sauce with butter, flour and milk. Season sauce with salt, pepper and nutmeg. Mix Swiss cheese and some milk into the sauce. Pour over artichokes, sprinkle with some more Swiss cheese plus some Parmesan sprinkled on top. Bake in a hot oven (375°) for about 20 minutes.   Serves 4-6.

ARTICHOKES CELLINI

1   package frozen artichoke
     hearts
1   small package (3 oz.)

Arrange artichokes close together in a single layer in a buttered, shallow baking dish (one you

cream cheese
1/4 cup chopped chives
1/4 cup soft butter or
margarine
Salt and pepper
1/2 cup shredded Parmesan
cheese

can serve from). Blend cream cheese with chives and butter. Sprinkle artichokes with salt and pepper and dot evenly with cheese mixture, then sprinkle evenly with Parmesan cheese (you can cover and chill dish at this point until ready to heat). Bake in moderately hot oven (375°) for 20 minutes or until cheese is golden.   Serves 4.

GRATIN COEURS D'ARTICHAUTS

1   package frozen artichoke
    hearts
2   tbsp. butter
2   tbsp. flour
1   tsp. garlic salt
2   cups rich milk
1/2 cup grated Parmesan
    cheese

Cook artichokes according to package directions. Generously butter flat baking dish, and arrange hearts evenly. Render butter in a pan and rub in flour until quite smooth. Gradually add milk, continuing to stir until very smooth. Add garlic salt and grated Parmesan cheese. Stir until well blended and pour over the artichoke hearts. Set dish under the broiler until nicely browned. Serve immediately.   Serves 6.

STUFFED CARDUUS

4   medium artichokes
2/3 cup fine dry bread crumbs
1   tsp. grated Parmesan
    cheese
1   tbsp. plus 1 tsp. chopped
    parsley
1   tsp. salt
3/4 tsp. pepper
2   cups water
2   tbsp. olive oil
    Garlic powder

Prepare whole artichokes for stuffing according to Method 1. Blend bread crumbs, cheese, 1 tsp. parsley, salt and pepper. Place mixture between leaves. Stand artichokes in skillet; add water, 1 tbsp. parsley and olive oil. Cook uncovered, for 30 minutes or until tender. To eat, pull out leaves one by one.

Serves 4.

CARCIOFI UMIDO

16 small artichokes
2   tbsp. olive oil
1   large onion, chopped
1   clove garlic, minced or

Prepare artichokes according to Method 2. Heat oil in a frying pan and add onion, tomato, garlic, basil, salt, pepper, water and

mashed
1/2 tsp. basil
3/4 tsp. salt
1/4 tsp. pepper
1/2 cup water
Grated or shredded Parmesan cheese

thoroughly drained artichokes. Cover and simmer for 15 minutes or until artichokes are easily pierced. Sprinkle with cheese.

Serves 4.

STUFFED HALVES

2   large artichokes
8   thin garlic slices
   Salt to taste
4   tbsp. olive oil
2   tbsp. fine dry bread crumbs
2   tbsp. grated Romano cheese
1/4 cup water

Prepare artichokes according to Method 1. Cut in half lengthwise and remove core. Insert 2 garlic slices in each half; season with salt and pepper. Pour 1 tbsp. olive oil over each half. Mix together the bread crumbs and cheese, and place a tbsp. in the center of each artichoke half. Arrange in baking dish and pour water into the bottom of the pan. Bake, covered, in a hot oven (400°) for 15 minutes; remove cover, and bake 30 minutes longer, or until artichokes are tender. Serve warm.

Serves 4.

HEARTS AU GRATIN

1   package frozen artichoke hearts (cut in half or quarters)
1-1/2 cups sauce mornay
3   tbsp. grated Swiss cheese
1   tbsp. butter
1   cup sauteed mushrooms

Cook artichokes according to package direction. Make the sauce mornay. When the artichokes are done, combine them with sauteed mushrooms; spread ⅓ of the sauce in a buttered casserole dish and arrange the artichoke hearts and mushrooms over it. Pour on the rest of the sauce, sprinkle on the cheese, and dot with butter. About 30 minutes before serving, place in a 375° oven to heat through, long enough to brown the top of sauce lightly. Serve hot.

Serves 4.

Sauces

Cored artichokes served either hot or cold filled with a sauce of your choice and garnished with parsley are a wonderful idea as a salad. They can also be served whole with individual cups of seasoned butter for dunking.

For the more adventurous chef there are sauces to be served with entrees that will add a gourmet touch to any meal.

SAUCES FOR DIPS AND STUFFINGS

Hollandaise
Mustard Mayonnaise
Parsley-Sour Cream
Oyster
Horseradish Sour Cream
Egg
Almond
Italian Dressing
Remoulade
Nicoise
Curry Mayonnaise
Parmesan Butter
Garlic Mayonnaise
Bechamel
Drawn Butter
Mustard
Anchovy Dip
Tuna Dip
Bearnaise Sauce
Artichoke Dip

SEASONED BUTTERS FOR SAUTEED HEARTS OR DIPS

Brown Wine
Anchovy
Caviar
Garlic
Lobster
Lemon
Smoked Salmon
Tarragon
Herb

SAUCES WITH ENTRES

Sauce for Beef
Artichoke Gravy
Italian Sauce
Crochette Sauce
Artichoke Sauce

EASY HOLLANDAISE SAUCE

2   egg yolks
3   tbsp. boiling water
1/4 cup melted butter or
    margarine
1   tbsp. lemon juice
1/8 tsp. salt
    Dash cayenne
    Pepper

Beat egg yolks with fork in top of small double boiler. Stir in water, tbsp at a time, mixing thoroughly. Set into bottom of double boiler containing not more than ½-inch boiling water. Stirring rapidly, cook 2 to 3 minutes until thickened to soft custard consistency. Remove from heat immediately and slowly stir in melted butter, lemon juice and seasonings. Serve at once, o r keep hot over warm, not boiling water. Makes about 4 servings.

MUSTARD MAYONNAISE

1/2 cup mayonnaise
2   tsp. lemon juice
1   tsp. prepared mustard

Gradually blend lemon juice and mustard into mayonnaise. Serve hot or cold. Makes about ½ cup or 2 to 3 servings. Plain mayonnaise or a combination of mayonnaise and lemon juice is also delightful, especially with cold artichokes.

PARSLEY-SOUR CREAM SAUCE

1   cup sour cream
2   tbsp. chopped parsley
1/2 tsp. salt
1   tbsp. lemon juice

Stir together sour cream, chopped parsley, salt, and lemon juice. This sauce is best when made early in the day and refrigerated several hours before serving.

OYSTER DIP

1   tsp. chopped shallot
1   clove minced garlic
2   tsp. minced onion
1   oz. butter
1   tsp. curry powder
1   oz. dry sherry
1   dozen oysters with juice
1   cup heavy cream
2   tbsp. cornstarch
    Lemon juice
    Salt, white pepper, and

Lightly saute the shallot, garlic, and onion in the butter until soft but not brown. Add the curry powder and the sherry and simmer until slightly reduced. Put the oysters and their juice in an electric blender for 30 seconds. Add to the simmering sauce and bring to a boil. Simmer for only a minute or two and add the cream. Simmer for another minute or

monosodium glutamate

two. Mix the cornstarch with 2 tbsp. cold water and add, stirring, bit by bit. Since cornstarch thickens liquid instantly, you can tell when you have added enough. Thin to the desired "dunking" consistency with lemon juice, or, if you prefer, a little light cream, or both. Season to taste with salt, white pepper and monosodium glutamate.

HORSE RADISH SOUR CREAM SAUCE

1/4 tsp. prepared horseradish
(or more to taste)
1/2 tsp. salt
1/2 pint (1 cup) commercial
sour cream

In a small bowl, thoroughly blend horse radish and salt with sour cream. Makes enough for 6 artichokes.

EGG SAUCE

1 hard-boiled egg
3/4 cup commercial sour
cream
1/4 cup mayonnaise
1/2 tsp. each dill weed and
salt

In a small bowl, mash egg with a fork. Thoroughly blend in sour cream, mayonnaise, dill weed, and salt. Makes enough for 6 artichokes.

ALMOND MAYONNAISE

1 tsp. lemon juice
1 cup mayonnaise
1/3 cup finely chopped toasted
almonds

Blend lemon juice into mayonnaise. Chill. Just before serving, fold in finely chopped toasted almonds.

ITALIAN DRESSING

1/2 cup olive or salad oil
1/3 cup vinegar
2 tbsp. water
4 thin slices onion
1 tbsp. sugar
1 clove garlic, crushed
1/4 tsp. celery seed
1/2 tsp. salt
Dash pepper

Combine all ingredients.

Remoulade Sauce
Sauce Nicoise
Curry Mayonnaise

REMOULADE SAUCE

1	tsp. warm water
3/4	tsp. tarragon, crumbled
1/2	tsp. chervil
1	cup mayonnaise
1	tbsp. drained mashed capers
2	tsp. mustard
1/2	tsp. anchovy paste

Combine water, tarragon and chervil. Let stand 10 minutes. Blend herbs with mayonnaise, capers, mustard, and anchovy paste. Chill well.

SAUCE NICOISE

1-1/2	cups mayonnaise
1	can (6-oz.) tomato paste
1	tbsp. chopped chives
1/2	tsp. dried tarragon

Blend mayonnaise with tomato paste, chopped chives and tarragon. Chill. Makes enough for 8 artichokes.

PARMESAN BUTTER

1/2	cup (1 cube) soft butter
1/3	cup grated Parmesan cheese
1-1/2	tbsp. minced parsley

In the small bowl of your electric mixer, combine soft butter, grated Parmesan cheese, and minced parsley. Whip with mixer until blended and fluffy. Makes enough for 6 artichokes.

GARLIC MAYONNAISE

1	cup mayonnaise
1	clove garlic, mashed
	Paprika

Blend mayonnaise and garlic. Spoon into artichoke casings or use as a dip. Sprinkle with paprika. Makes enough for 6 artichokes.

BECHAMEL SAUCE

3	tbsp. butter
5	tbsp. all-purpose flour
2	cups milk (variable)
	Salt and pepper

Use a heavy metal saucepan. Cut the butter into pieces for uniform melting and heat over a moderate heat. Add all the flour at once and mix well with a wooden spoon, cooking for a few minutes until the mixture is pale gold. Too high a heat will brown the mixture. Remove the pan from the fire and pour in the cold milk. Stir well and put back on the fire, stirring until the mixture thickens. Season well. Pepper is indispensable to a good bechamel.

DRAWN BUTTER SAUCE

6 tbsp. butter
3 tbsp. flour
  Salt and pepper
1-1/2 cups of fish or vegetable stock
1 tsp. strained lemon juice

Melt butter (3 tbsp.) and blend in flour; season to taste with salt and pepper, and gradually add fish or vegetable stock, stirring constantly. Let boil gently for 5 minutes, then add bit by bit 3 more tbsp. of butter, still stirring gently, alternately with strained lemon juice. Appropriate for any kind of boiled, broiled or baked fish and vegetable.

MUSTARD SAUCE

4 tbsp. mayonnaise
2 tbsp. prepared mustard
1 tsp. minced Chervil
1/2 tsp. minced spearmint
1 tsp. minced chives

Mix ingredients thoroughly, and let stand 1 hour before serving.

BROWNED WINE BUTTER

1/2 cup butter
1/4 tsp. salt
  Dash cayenne
1/2 cup white wine

Heat butter till brown; stir in salt. cayenne, white wine. Serve hot. If wine is not desired, 2 tbsp.of lemon juice may be substituted.

ANCHOVY BUTTER

2 tbsp. sweet butter
  Anchovy paste, the size of a hazelnut

Pound or cream sweet butter with anchovy paste, use more or less according to taste.

CAVIAR BUTTER

1 tbsp. black caviar
2 tbsp. sweet butter

Pound caviar until fine. Place in a fine cloth and twist to remove the oily liquid and briny water, then cream with sweet butter and chill.

GARLIC BUTTER

1 clove of garlic
1 tbsp. salt butter

Blanch clove of garlic in a very little water. Drain, dry, then cream or pound with butter. Chill.

LOBSTER BUTTER
1 tbsp. lobster trimmings
2 tbsp. salt butter

Pound or ground several times, the lobster trimmings such as: coral, milky meat, roe, and so forth, with salt butter. Chill.

LEMON BROWNED BUTTER
1/2 cup butter
3 tbsp. lemon juice
1/3 tsp. Worcestershire sauce

Brown butter and add Worcestershire sauce with lemon juice.

SMOKED SALMON BUTTER
2 tbsp. sweet butter
1 tsp. smoked salmon paste

Cream sweet butter with salmon paste. More or less paste may be used in accordance with your taste. (Almost all smoked fish may be used in this manner.)

TARRAGON BUTTER
1 tsp. tarragon leaves, fresh or dried
2 tbsp. salt butter

Pound, then rub tarragon leaves through a fine-meshed sieve, cream with salt butter, blending thoroughly. Then rub through a fine-meshed sieve. Chill.

ANCHOVY DIP
1 package (3 oz.) cream cheese
1 can (2 oz.) flat anchovies, drain and chopped
2 tbsp. lemon juice
2 tbsp. mayonnaise
1 tsp. dehydrated minced onion

Combine all ingredients and mix well.

TUNA DIP
1/2 cup instant nonfat dry milk crystals
1/2 cup water
1/2 tsp. salt
1/4 to 1/2 tsp. instant minced garlic
1/4 tsp. soy sauce
Dash pepper

Stir instant crystals into water. Add seasonings, blend in cottage cheese and tuna. Serve with artichokes. Makes about 2 cups.

1   cup (8 oz.) uncreamed
    cottage cheese
1   can (6½ oz.) dietetic tuna,
    drained

BEARNAISE SAUCE

4   egg yolks
    Juice of 1 lemon
2   cups melted butter
    Salt and pepper
2   tbsp. capers
1/4 cup chopped parsley
1   tbsp. tarragon vinegar

In top half of double boiler, beat egg yolks and lemon juice. Cook slowly over very low heat, never allowing water in bottom pan to come to a boil. Slowly add melted butter to above mixture, stirring constantly with a wooden spoon. Add salt, pepper (to taste), capers, parsley and vinegar. Stir to blend. Makes 2 cups.

ARTICHOKE DIP

1   jar of artichoke hearts
1   small onion, chopped fine
1   clove garlic, crushed
1   tbsp. olive oil
2   tbsp. lemon juice
1   tomato, peeled and diced
1/4 tsp. salt
1/8 tsp. pepper
1   anchovy fillet

Place hearts in blender for 30 seconds, leave slightly lumpy. Add other ingredients. Mix well. Serve on crackers or as a dip.

WHIPPED HERB BUTTER

1/2 cup (1 cube) soft butter
1-1/2 to 2 tbsp. lemon juice
1/2 tsp. chervil
1/4 tsp. each rosemary and
    tarragon

In the small bowl of your electric mixer, combine soft butter, lemon juice, chervil, rosemary and tarragon. Whip with the mixer until blended and fluffy. Makes enough for 6 artichokes.

ARTICHOKE SAUCE FOR BEEF

1/4 cup butter
1   package frozen artichoke
    hearts, thawed
    All meat juices
1   cup burgundy
2/3 cup ruby port
2   beef bouillon cubes

Melt butter in small skillet; saute artichoke hearts until golden. Reserve. Remove all but two tbsp. fat from meat juices in roasting pan. Combine burgundy, port, bouillon cubes, onion powder, fines herbes, garlic powder,

1-1/2 tsp. onion powder
1 tsp. fines herbes
1/8 tsp. garlic powder
1/8 tsp. ground cloves
1/8 tsp. orange peel
1-1/2 tbsp. cornstarch
1 cup water

ARTICHOKE GRAVY

2 tbsp. olive oil
2 tbsp. butter or margarine
1/2 medium size onion, chopped
1 clove garlic, minced
1 tbsp. minced parsley
3 artichoke hearts, chopped
1 can (8 oz.) Spanish style tomato sauce
1/2 cup water
Salt and pepper

ITALIAN SAUCE

1/2 cup chopped mushrooms
1 tbsp. olive oil
1/4 cup minced lean ham
1 shallot, chopped or green onion
1/2 cup white wine
2 tbsp. tomato puree
1 cup beef gravy
1 tsp. minced parsley

CROCHETTE SAUCE

2 jars marinated artichoke hearts
2 tsp. salt
1/2 tsp. pepper
1 (14½ oz.) can tomatoes
1 (4 oz.) can sliced mushrooms and liquid
2 cans tomato sauce (8 oz.)
1-1/2 tsp. crushed oregano

cloves, and orange peel. Stir into meat juices. Boil until liquid is reduced to one half. Blend cornstarch into water. Add to pan liquid, stirring constantly. Strain. Stir in reserved sauteed artichoke hearts. Heat two to three minutes longer. Serve immediately with beef.

Heat oil and butter in heavy frying pan. Stir in onion and fry until lightly browned. Add garlic, parsley, and chopped artichoke hearts, and fry slowly. Add tomato sauce, water, salt and pepper to taste. Cook slowly for 1 hour or until thick. Meat may be added if desired. Serves 6 with spaghetti, tagliarini or veal cutlets.

Brown mushrooms in olive oil. Add ham and shallot or green onion; cook 3 minutes. Add wine, boil quickly to reduce to one-half, then add tomato puree and beef gravy. Simmer 5 minutes, add minced parsley, and serve. Makes 2 cups.

Combine all ingredients, cutting artichoke hearts into smaller pieces or separating leaves. Simmer until thick. Serve over spaghetti, top with Parmesan cheese and pieces of crab meat.

1/4 tsp. garlic powder
1 tbsp. minced onion
1 tbsp. sugar
1 cup water
1 tsp. thyme
1/2 tsp. monosodium gulta-
mate
1 bay leaf
1 tbsp. parsley flakes

ARTICHOKE SAUCE

1 jar marinated artichoke
hearts
1 can white sauce or
1-1/2 cups prepared white
sauce
Potato chips

In blender puree the artichoke hearts along with the oil. Add moisture to white sauce. Heat sauce and use in any of the following ways:

Spread sauce over fish, place under broiler and cook until fish is flaky. Remove from broiler, spread a second light covering of the sauce and crumbled potato chips. Return to broiler until chips are lightly browned.

Use over rice or noodles, combining sauce with shrimp or crab.